A PRIEST ON TRIAL

A PRIEST ON TRIAL

FATHER BERNARD LYNCH

BLOOMSBURY

First published in Great Britain 1993

Bloomsbury Publishing Limited, 2 Soho Square,
London W1V 5DE

'A Priest on Trial' is the title of a Channel 4
television documentary about Father Lynch
written and directed by Conor McAnally

The extract from *Waiting for Godot* by Samuel
Beckett on page ix is reproduced by kind
permission of Faber and Faber Limited

Certain names of people and places have been changed,
to protect the innocent and the not so innocent

A CIP catalogue record for this book
is available from the British Library

ISBN 0 7475 1036 9

Typeset by Hewer Text Composition Services, Edinburgh
Printed in England by Clays Limited, St Ives plc, Bungay, Suffolk

For:
My father, John Lynch;
My Provincial, Father Cornelius Murphy, and
his administration.

In memory of:
My mother, Kitty Lynch;
My brother, Sean;
And all my friends who have died of AIDS.

And with heartfelt thanks
to my family of friends who stood by me.

ACKNOWLEDGEMENTS

I would like to be able to name all of those who made my survival through the story behind *A Priest on Trial* possible. The dedication 'to my family of friends who stood by me' is an attempt to do this in spirit if not in word.

As in any event of this magnitude, some people naturally paid a higher price than others for their fidelity and friendship. I would, then, in addition to those named in the dedication, like to list some of those without whose love and support I would not have survived:

Father Laurence Wrenne and his parish priest Father Michael Crowley, Conor McAnally, Bishop Paul Moore, Charles Frederick, Michael Mulligan, Sister Jorinne Cieciuch, Sister Karen Killeen, Dignity New York and Dignity AIDS ministry, Brian McDermott, Pat Cooney, Winifred Warner, Mary Lynch and the Monday-night group, Joe and Anne Ford, Tony Cataldo, Kate Charters, Father Martin Reynolds, Father Jim Cotter, Father John Lee and his wife Sue, my aunt Ethna Dardis and my sister Thérèse Lynch Lawton and her husband Charles . . . and the late Eileen O'Neill Androvette, my ninety-two-years-young cousin . . . *Go raibh mile maith agaibh.*

To Mike Petty, David Reynolds, Mark Lucas and Penny Phillips, my grateful thanks for helping me to get this book together. And my gratitude also to Michael Kennedy and Bob Cammer, who were hired as my defence attorneys and, together with Michael's wife Eleanora, became my friends. I celebrate you for restoring my faith in the system.

CONTENTS

Let us not waste our time in idle discourse! . . . Let us do something while we have the chance! It is not every day that we are needed. Not indeed that we personally are needed. Others would meet the challenge equally well, if not better. To all humankind they were addressed, those cries for help still ringing in our ears! But at this place, at this moment of time, all mankind is us, whether we like it or not . . . What we are doing here, *that* is the question. And we are blessed in this, that we happen to know the answer. Yes, in this immense confusion one thing alone is clear: we are waiting for Godot to come − . . . or for night to fall. We have kept our appointment and that's an end to that. We are not saints, but we have kept our appointment. How many people can boast as much?

SAMUEL BECKETT, *Waiting for Godot*

Prologue

'Bernard, put your pants back on, right now. And you, Michael Ragott. Wait till Father Queeley hears about this!'

Thirty-seven years on, my mother's voice came back to me as I stood before Judge Burton Roberts in the Bronx Supreme Court, listening to the clerk's voice droning out the hideous words of the indictment: '. . . accuse the defendant of the crime of sexual abuse in the first degree . . .'

I was terribly anxious and afraid; I had had plenty of time to get used to the idea that I, Father Bernard Lynch, was to be tried for the sexual abuse of a minor, but I still could not believe it was happening to me. It was as if I was having an out-of-body experience. *I* knew I was innocent, and my attorney, Michael Kennedy, was one of the best in the business. My family and friends all knew I was innocent. But when the trial was over, would the Judge believe I was innocent?

I had returned voluntarily to New York to face the charges, and today, Thursday June 23, 1988, was the day of my arrest and arraignment. My friend Winifred Warner had picked me up at my apartment and driven me into the unfamiliar territory of the South Bronx. I couldn't help remembering, as we passed Yankee Stadium, that the last time I'd been there was to concelebrate mass with the Pope. I doubted whether he'd be showing up today.

1

I met Michael Kennedy on the courthouse steps at 8 a.m., and he led me down into the holding room. I'd been in a police precinct before, on behalf of the occasional student who'd got into trouble with the law, but in all my time living in the city I'd never got so much as a traffic ticket. Now I was in a room full of armed cops and what looked like hardened criminals, men who, if I did go to jail, would make a sexual scapegoat of me. I knew that men convicted of sexual crimes against minors are regarded as the lowest of the low even by murderers.

Detective Gelfand, the arresting officer, and FBI Agents Clementi and McDonald stood around me as the desk sergeant asked the formal questions – name, age, address, occupation and so on. Someone said, 'You don't have to handcuff him, he's given himself up voluntarily.'

I was taken to another room where I was fingerprinted and photographed, and asked to turn out my pockets. I was treated with great courtesy, but as I watched them leafing carefully through my diary I realised that I no longer had any privacy – my life belonged to the Supreme Court of the County of the Bronx.

Gelfand and McDonald stayed with me as we waited to be called to court. The day wore on interminably. I tried to read the book I'd brought with me, the life of St Teresa of Avila, but the words made no sense to me. When I went to the bathroom Detective Gelfand came with me, and insisted that I left the stall door open in case I tried to escape. Still, I don't suppose he enjoyed it any more than I did.

We could not go to the court until my fingerprints and photograph had been checked in the State capital at Albany. It eventually became apparent, after even more hours had dragged by, that there had been a foulup somewhere along the line and clearance was not going to be forthcoming. So it was decided that we'd just go to court anyway. As we made our way to the sixth floor of the courthouse building I was constantly greeted – 'Hello, Father', 'Hola, Padre' –

by people assuming that I was going to court to speak for some criminal or other.

I shall never forget the sight of the dozens of supporters crowded into the public seats of the oak-panelled courtroom, representatives from all periods of my thirteen years in New York City. There were friends and neighbours from my first assignment at St Gabriel's in the Bronx, boys (now young men) from St Gabriel's grammar school, former students from Mount St Michael's Academy (including two police officers in full uniform), nuns and priests, members of Dignity and Integrity (respectively Catholic and Episcopal gay/lesbian organisations), people with AIDS (PWAs) . . . As the court officer opened the door for me the entire crowd stood in respectful silence, as though I was approaching the altar to celebrate mass. I went weak at the knees, and had to choke back the tears.

And so it all began. Emblazoned on the panelling above the Judge's head were the words 'In God We Trust'. As the indictment was read out I wondered if I did really believe in God any more, at any rate the God of institutional religion.

How had that naughty little boy with no trousers on ended up in this terrible predicament?

PART I

THE MAKING OF A PRIEST

Chapter
One

My mother was always sick in the morning. I didn't know why, but somehow I always felt responsible. There were many pregnancies: nine in all. I was the eldest of the six that survived, three boys and three girls.

But the early years were happy ones. There was only my brother Sean and I. (The second baby, Joseph, died at birth.) Even so, by the time I made my first communion at the age of seven I knew I was different, not the boy I seemed. In primary school the teacher – a friend of my dad's – chose me to captain the class hurling team. The shame and disgrace I brought on my family when I scored an own goal! I was called a sissy, a girl, an eejit. It was only the first of many dents in my self-image. The Christian Brothers' school was typical of west of Ireland primary schools of its day. I had spent three blissful years in pre-primary with the nuns, and entering an all-male school was traumatic. It was as if I knew instinctively that it was no place for my androgynous soul to flourish.

I had had, of course, no sexual education of any kind, other than what I picked up on the streets from other boys. I thought babies were delivered by plane to Shannon airport, or found under a bush in Sheehan's back garden. When I discovered what my parents had been up to I couldn't believe they'd do such a thing. My sense of what was appropriate was even further skewed during these years by my membership of not one, but two rather Jansenistic religious groups.

The Dominic Savio Club was designed to safeguard our bodily purity. It was strictly forbidden even to look at a man and a woman kissing on a movie screen. The Brother in charge instructed us that taking pleasure in an erection was a venial sin. Since from pubescence on I had a more or less permanent erection, my mortal soul was clearly in some danger. I tried applying holy water and my miraculous medal to my stubborn penis, but to no avail. I said novenas, prayed the rosary, went to daily mass and communion, but still my 'teapot', as the nuns used to call it in pre-primary, insisted on spouting.

In the Legion of Mary presidium, on the other hand, we were instructed by the local chaplain and curate to be on the lookout for evil literature, which mostly found its way to our town through that pagan gateway, Shannon airport. Evil literature was defined as that which displayed any part of a woman's anatomy above the knees or below the neck. The priest need not have worried on my account; with my fast-developing attraction towards members of my own gender, I was out of reach of the sort of evil literature he had in mind. Part of our Legion work consisted of countering the menace by the sale of Holy Books, particularly those dealing with purity. Every market-day – Saturday in Ennis – we would set up a six-by-four wooden hut outside the church, stocked with such improving titles as *The Devil at Dances*, *What a Boy Should Know*, *What a Girl Should Know*, *Modern Youth and Chastity* and *Purity, the Queen of Virtues*. The two innocent faces visible above the counter, against a backdrop of Holy Books, were in stark contrast to the sex play that went on below the counter, invisible to the faithful shoppers and farmers. The schizophrenic guilt induced by this behaviour can easily be imagined. It was only a mutual infatuation with another boy of my own age, and our mutual resolve to be pure, that allowed me to suppress my unruly libido and channel it into further religious activity.

In all my eleven years with the Christian Brothers my favourite teacher was Brother Widecell, a wizened little man with a wicked temper, widely known for feeling up the boys. He took a liking to me, and made the lucky discovery that I had a remarkably good singing voice. I was drafted into the Operetta Society, and soon developed fantasies of becoming the Caruso of Ennis. Being given the lead role was no small thing for a lad from St Michael's villas; they usually went to boys from the better part of town, even though some of them had the range of a castrated crow. Sometimes their solos had to be given to the soprano – me – because I was the only one who could carry them. My parents, already bursting with pride, fell to arguing over which side of the family my talent came from.

My father drove a horse and cart round the streets of Ennis for a living, delivering goods sent by rail from Dublin. I remember gleefully sitting beside him on one occasion after a triumph in the school operetta and a rave review in the *Clare Champion*. I never felt closer to him in my entire childhood than then, as my father admitted to all and sundry that, yes, I was the newly discovered boy soprano and he was my Dad. He gave me half a crown, and told me that both he and Mum were truly proud of me. For the moment at least, the hurling fiasco was forgotten.

At the final performance later in the week, attended by Bishop Rogers, each lead actor was to receive a box of chocolates from his family. My parents could not afford such luxuries, but it was important not to lose face. So my mother took the large empty chocolate box that stood in front of the fireplace in my parents' bedroom like a screen, wrapped it neatly, and presented it to me in grand fashion, alongside the no-patches-on-their-trousers boys from the better side of town. All went according to plan until the boys from the chorus descended on me like locusts, intent on reminding me which side of town *I* came from. I hung on to my empty box for dear life, calling on every saint in heaven to protect me from humiliation at the hands of my own. I was saved by the providential arrival of my mother and her sister at the stage door. Mum immediately sized up the situation and took charge of the chocolate box, at the same time distracting the boys with sweets from her pockets.

There is a saying in Ireland that priests are born not made, and this was certainly true of me – I cannot remember a time when I did not want to be a priest. Even before I joined the altar boys at the age of eight I had played at saying Mass, and always had an altar to Jesus, Mary or one or other of the saints in my bedroom. In May every year I would festoon my room with blue and white crepe paper and bundles of wild flowers to honour the Blessed Virgin Mary. I almost burned the house down once, when on November 3, the Feast of St Martin de Porres, I left a candle burning in front of his picture, and the streamers I had arranged round my altar caught fire.

It is difficult in this day and age to give an accurate impression of what the Church meant to us young lads as we grew up. Where I lived nobody could afford carpet on the floor, and we used to try and sneak into the local hotel, a posh place called the Old Ground, just so that we could walk on the carpet before the porter chased us out again. The church provided a sacred space where we could feast our eyes on carpet. The sanctuary of the pro-cathedral church had a deep green carpet, with decorative patterns woven into it, and every Sunday my eyes would melt with envy as I watched the priest float, as it were, around the space behind the altar rails, going about God's business.

In those pre-Vatican II days, no one was allowed behind the rails but priest, sacristan and altar boys. Everything behind those rails was magic. God was there in his golden box, the Tabernacle. The altar was covered with starched white linen cloths, three huge brass candlesticks, and beautiful brass vases full of flowers. In fact, and in fancy, this was an escape from the realities of life.

The Bishop and the priests of our parish were good men, devoted to the Church and to the people. Although they could be strict sometimes, they never abused us, unlike the Christian Brothers. The Bishop, Dr Rogers, was a lordly type, rather corpulent, but very kind. Because I was an especially good altar boy, I was often lucky enough to be asked to serve him, or to sit on a footstool beside his throne when he attended services.

On one such occasion the Bishop asked me to hold his pink biretta during the intonation of the 'Gloria'. I put it on his throne, whereupon he sat on it. I can still hear the giggles from the congregation as the Bishop turned crimson and rescued the completely flattened headgear from beneath him. My family, proudly in attendance, prayed for the ground to open up beneath them, while I yet again invoked all the saints to prevent me from wetting my pants. As he went on his rounds the next day my Dad had to put up with some pretty heavy-handed compliments about how his lad had made the Bishop sit on his hat.

Becoming an altar boy, then, was a first step towards respectability, as well as the first blossoming of my priestly vocation. Quite simply, I loved the church. There, I felt secure, loved and accepted; there was order, and everything was in its place, and everyone was gentle and kind. I could be close to God in the Tabernacle, and every time it was my turn to cover the altar with the cloth, I would whisper, 'Jesus, I love you!' into the Tabernacle door. I really believed He heard me, cared for me, and understood me as no one else did. I still do.

Chapter
Two

With the opening of the Irish state-owned television station, R.T.E., in the 1960s, the outside world arrived in Ennis with a vengeance. My father – for educational purposes, he informed us – decided that we should become the very first family in St Michael's Villas to own a television. Sixty children or more would squeeze into our kitchen in the afternoons, waiting for the test card to disappear and Kathleen Watkins to announce *Rin-Tin-Tin*. My mother would nestle by the fire, one eye on the screen and the other on the crowd, making sure that they all appreciated the honour that was being done them. In the past visits to the Gaiety cinema had only grudgingly been allowed, and it was very hard to avoid giving myself airs at the distinction that had been conferred on me.

Of course, in a town the size of Ennis – around 8,000 – knowing your place was of the utmost importance, and there were plenty of people willing to make sure you knew it if you got above yourself. The first woman on our block to work as an air hostess for Aer Lingus (the peak of working-class ambition), was bluntly reminded of her roots as she swaggered by with her nose in the air. 'Look at the arse on that one – you'd swear she never shit in a bucket!' came the cry from a local shopkeeper.

I was forcibly reminded of my status when, at the age

of thirteen or fourteen, I tried to gain admission to the Redemptorist Juniorate, a secondary school run by the Redemptorist Fathers for those interested in joining their religious community. As usual, I was not thinking of any vocation other than the priesthood, my ambition fuelled even more by the movie of Henry Morton Robinson's book *The Cardinal*, very popular around this time. To my distress, I was rejected by the school because my parents could not afford the fees.

I always wore hand-me-down long pants, passed on by relatives in New York. It is no wonder that, of all the vocation priests who recruited in my final years at Ennis Christian Brothers' School, the one who impressed me most had a patch on his trousers. We had priests from Florida offering cars and vacations if we would come and serve in their diocese, priests from California offering trips to Disneyland, but this down-at-heel man, inviting us to work with the poor in Africa, won my admiration and respect; he came from my own class, I felt.

So it was that I joined the Society of African Missions (S.M.A.). I had no particular dedication to black people; indeed, I had never seen one. In fact when our neighbour Mrs Mahoney went to hospital for an operation, she had us all praying to the black saint and patron of the sick, Martin de Porres – 'Blessed' Martin at the time. She thought she had died and gone to heaven when she awoke from the anaesthetic and saw at the end of her bed the young Nigerian doctor who was doing an internship at the hospital in Ennis. 'St Martin!' she exclaimed. 'Jesus, help me, You did not answer my prayer!'

Africa was far from the heart and mind of the eighteen-year-old would-be novice as I boarded my train for Galway City on September 15, 1965. I was headed for the S.M.A. novitiate at Cloughballymore, in the boondocks of Galway. There were twenty-six of us that first year, and in truth it was as if we were starting a wondrous adventure.

Certainly it was the best year of my life. We were cut

off completely from the outside world in our monastic life of *labor et ora*; no visitors, no radio, no television, no newspapers. Our mail, both incoming and outgoing, was censored. The will of the superior was the will of God, and we firmly believed that. Every minute of our day was programmed:

6 a.m.: Rise
6.20: Morning prayer and meditation
7.00: Mass
7.30: Thanksgiving
7.45: Housework
8.15: Breakfast
8.45: Recreation
9.10: Class
10.50: Break
11.00: Class
12.45: Particular examination of conscience
1.00: Lunch
1.45: Break
2.15: Work or games
4.00: Afternoon tea
4.30: Spiritual reading
5.30: Rosary and meditation
6.00: High tea
7.00: Study
9.00: Break
9.30: Night prayer
10.00: Lights out

Above all, we were taught obedience. Our novicemaster, the Reverend Tom Egan, a holy but rather neurotic man, insisted that if he requested us to do something, whether it was cleaning the stairs from the bottom up or planting cabbages upside-down, then that was the will of God. The bell which brought us to every exercise, and also told us when it was completed, was referred to as 'the Voice of God'. The sacristan would ring the bell first thing in the morning with the cry, '*Benedicamus Domino*!', to which the appropriate response was, '*Deo Gratias*!' On more than one occasion the response was an entirely inappropriate 'Fuck off!', to thunderous applause from all round the dormitory.

We had a thirty-day retreat at the beginning of our novitiate year, and an eight-day retreat at the end, with many other shorter retreats in between. (Much later, when I heard about the Moonies' indoctrination process, I couldn't help reflecting on the similarities to our own!) After our final retreat, in June 1966, I was admitted into the pious Society of African Missions, and took my first oath in religious life: to be obedient to my superiors for one year. The oath was administered by the Provincial of the Order, the Very Reverend Dr John A. Craven, most nervously assisted by Father Egan. We had been preparing for months for this important occasion, painting, cleaning, manicuring the lawns, dressing the flowerbeds, and the novitiate was in tiptop condition, both inside and out. Dr Craven's presence heightened our awareness of how auspicious this celebration was. In a sense we felt we were being admitted to some exclusive and secret society, though through little merit of our own.

My father and my brother Sean were at Ennis station to meet me when I arrived home for the first time in ten months. My mother waited back at the house, and I can still see her eyes filling with tears as she kissed me and welcomed me back after what seemed like an interminable absence. The house felt tiny, after the institutional atmosphere of the novitiate. To my amazement, there was one major difference: the stairs were carpeted! A carpet factory had opened in Ennis, and a relative was auditing their books. As a result, some offcuts had made their way to our stairs, just in time for the homecoming of the young priest-to-be.

My brothers and sisters did not know what to make of me; I felt like a fish out of water. I was their brother, on my way to becoming a priest, yet I was no longer the brother

I once was. Nor yet was I a priest. Never again was I to feel the same, or be treated the same, as my siblings. I was different, doubly so; different by orientation (though my sexuality remained repressed and suppressed), and now, most of all, different by vocation. The church was now not only my home from home, it was my true home. That first summer we were forbidden by our superiors to work, presumably in case our sacred calling was defiled in some way. And so, every morning, I would trot off to church with my meditation book and mass missal, looking like an accident waiting to happen.

Chapter
Three

In the autumn of 1966 I entered our major seminary, African Missions College at Dromantine, Newry, County Down. This beautiful old neo-classical mansion, some twenty-six miles from Belfast, was idyllically set amongst rolling hills, with its own freshwater lake and farm. I was to remain here for six years, studying philosophy and theology, preparing myself for my eventual ordination to the priesthood.

I found myself in a hermetically sealed world, forbidden by the rules of the college to have any contact whatsoever with outsiders. There were about 120 students in all, ranging in age from eighteen to twenty-six. Twelve priests and ten lay people were in residence, along with nuns and a lay religious brother to care for our physical well-being. With our own shop, post office and credit union, our insulation was complete.

The hierarchical structure was Victorian in its rigidity. Every student and every staff member had his place, and did not dare venture outside it. The pecking order applied to everything, down to the most menial housekeeping jobs; we 'philosophers', being junior to the theologians, were required to clean their toilets. Above the theologians were the priests, known as 'gods'. Close contact with one's superiors, whether theologians or staff, was forbidden, which naturally served to increase the awe in which we held some of the professors.

I was a serious student, absolutely delighted with intellectual stimulation of any kind. The seminary, in stark contrast to my experience in primary and secondary school, invited us to learn rather than rammed learning down our throats. The professors were a mixed bag, academically speaking – as in any other institution of higher learning – and every one was a gentleman to his fingertips. Men like Doctor Robert Molloy, Fathers Jackie Power and John Quinlan, were above average both in what they taught us and the skill with which they communicated their subjects to us. We had classes in everything from ontology to epistemology, from ethics to missiography, from Christology to English literature. The atmosphere was happy, though highly controlled and somewhat greenhouse-like; in the practical sense, of course, our courses provided very little preparation for what was to come.

Tragically, the sexual education dispensed in the seminary was only one step above what you got on the street corners of Ennis. We were lectured at great length on the symbolic and practical value of celibacy, but there was simply no humanistic, psychological approach to sexuality. Most of the Fathers had little to offer on this most basic and fundamental way of being human. I well remember the Spiritual Director lecturing us on celibacy and ordination on one occasion, and informing us that impotence was a canonical impediment to ordination. One of my fellow students asked him, quite sincerely, to explain exactly what impotence was. After a great deal of blushing and stammering, the best he could come up with was: 'If a bomb went off between your legs you would be impotent.' It didn't seem to have occurred to him that if a bomb went off between your legs impotence would be the least of your problems.

Our sexual growth was frustrated, and so, inevitably, was our growth as human beings. Any conversation about sex always foundered on the rocks of what was right and what was wrong. For aspirants to the priesthood anything to do with sex was wrong. There was no way out. It was assumed by the authorities, and accepted for the most part by the students, that we would have no relations of any kind with the opposite sex. Indeed, such activity was considered a *de facto* admission that there was no vocation, practically a sign from God that He didn't want us as priests. Nothing, ironically enough, was said about same-sex relationships.

Homosexuality was not, as some might expect, rampant in the seminary. The fact that close physical contact was forbidden meant that everyone was on his guard; the love that dare not speak its name dared not speak at all. Inevitably, in a closed society of sexually aware young males, relationships developed, timid and covert at first. In my novitiate year I had made friends with Alex, a young man my own age, and by the second seminary year our relationship had become sexual, albeit at a very innocent level. We were both 'jocks', keen on cross-country, football, training together and so on, and derived our sexual gratification from giving each other massages.

Like any other students we had long summer vacations, but we were not allowed to take manual jobs unless they were of an apostolic nature. By the third summer my pal and I decided that we'd had enough of apostolic work, and the impoverished idleness that followed, so we headed off on our own to work in England, that country of 'paganism and religionlessness', as the Christian Brothers used to say. We worked happily together in a factory in Liverpool, the city jocularly known as the capital of Ireland on account of its large immigrant population. We lodged in a boarding house run by an Irish nurse, a spinster, and we had no difficulty with her request that we sleep in the one bed. Indeed, neither of us had ever had a bed to himself apart from our three years with the Society. Such a luxury was unknown in large families. Naturally nature ran its course, and we became more sexually involved. I felt sufficiently guilty about the situation to confess to a local priest, without in any way believing that I was putting my ordination to priesthood in danger.

But the priest, a devout Englishman, clearly felt otherwise. Shocked to the core, he refused to absolve me unless I promised never to have sexual dealings with my friend again, and to report the incident to the authorities on my return to the seminary. In my innocence I did not realise that this last condition was a breach of the canonical seal, but I agreed anyway, so desperate was I for absolution. I was too embarrassed to tell my friend what had happened.

On our return to the seminary – I had turned twenty-one by this time – I elected to speak to Father Jeremy Mullins. He was on the staff of the college, but I had never before had any reason to approach this awesome man, recognised as a brilliant academic both in Ireland and abroad. Nevertheless, he had the reputation of being approachable; he was considerate, compassionate and – it was said – generous to a fault. So it was, when it seemed that my whole world was about to come crashing down about me, that I met the man who would ultimately determine my destiny for many years to come.

I found a man boxed in by his own yearnings, sitting chain-smoking before the fire.

'I've been doing something with another student,' I blurted. 'We've . . . touched each other.'

'How long?'

'Over a year now.'

'What made you come and tell me now?'

I told Father Mullins about the priest in Liverpool. He was sympathetic, but I could see that he was tense.

'Celibacy is very hard, and it's no easier when you get older,' he said at last. 'I'm afraid you'll have to leave.'

I went into total shock.

'Not at once. You can have six weeks to tell your parents and make your arrangements. If you leave three weeks apart, it will not be obvious why you're both leaving.'

I found my voice. 'You can't ask me to leave. I'm a *priest*

. . . I have my collar, and my soutane . . . my *vocation* . . .'
– and I started crying.

I knew he understood, but he was inflexible. 'It's the rule,' he said.

My world had fallen apart. I was convinced that it was God's will that I should be a priest; I knew I had always been a priest in my heart, and that this was something the Church merely had to recognise, not give me. But I was equally convinced that what I had been doing was not wrong. After all, I reasoned naïvely with myself, Jesus loved his beloved disciple John, and I loved Alex. Of course Jesus didn't have sex with John, but he was divine, and I was human. Neither of us could understand what was wrong about mutual masturbation. So innocent were we, indeed, that when Father Mullins asked us if we had entered each other from behind, neither of us knew what he was talking about. Our ignorance about homosexual behaviour was sublime.

Alex, not surprisingly, was extremely angry with me for letting this particular cat out of the bag, and this only added to my torment. I lay awake at night wondering how on earth I was even going to tell my parents, much less make them understand. Thank God, reason prevailed, and a week later Father Mullins relented.

'I haven't brought it up with the Council. I want to give you and Alex a second chance,' he said. Seminarians were not in fact vowed to celibacy until their deaconate, and although that did not strictly speaking cover this case, it was good enough for Father Mullins.

Years later, I received a call from Father Mullins at my rectory in New York. He admitted that the reason he had given us another chance was that he was himself plagued by similar thoughts and desires.

Chapter
Four

Alex and I resolved never again to confess our relationship to anyone, at least until we were well and truly into the 'club' and ordained ourselves. But the celibacy issue weighed more and more heavily on Alex, and he finally decided in the spring of 1971 to leave, ten months before ordination.

I was broken-hearted when my friend left. I felt that all the prayers and spiritual exercises in the world could not compensate for his love and companionship, and eventually I suggested to Alex that I too was willing to leave if he and I could settle somewhere as a couple. Gay liberation was a long way from our minds – we had not even heard the word 'gay' used in that context, and had no idea that there might be others on the planet like us. I consulted a well-known counsellor, who was also an Agony Aunt in a national newspaper, and soon realised that he was almost as ignorant of the subject as we were.

In the end, however, with the help of a spiritual director (outside the seminary, naturally) I decided that it was God's will that I should now be ordained. In the wake of Alex's departure I could contemplate celibacy with something like equanimity, and I was ordained a deacon in June 1971, taking my perpetual oath in the Society of African Missions.

This was the final step before the priesthood. I could

now do everything a priest does, except forgive sins and celebrate mass. For the first time I was allowed to wear the Roman collar in public. At home in Ennis my parents, my grandparents, even my beloved grand-uncle and his house-keeper, greeted me with a sumptuous feast to celebrate my ordination to deaconate. My maternal grandfather was the least enthusiastic of my relatives about my priestly vocation – he had witnessed the civil war in Ireland at first hand, and had seen people he knew and respected excommunicated for their part in the struggle for independence. He therefore took a cautious and somewhat cynical attitude to church power. But my father's eyes glowed with pride as we tucked in to the spread.

On the following Sunday I was allowed to distribute holy communion in our local church, the pro-cathedral of Saints Peter and Paul. There was a traffic jam in the aisles as members of our extended family and our neighbours jostled and elbowed each other to be the first to receive communion from 'our Bernard'. My grandmother, in fact, refused communion from the priest ahead of me and stubbornly held her ground until her grandson came by to place the sacred host on her tongue.

That summer I hitch-hiked around Europe, and, by grace and effort, my celibacy was no big deal. All thoughts of other choices, or settling into a relationship, were forgotten. I was now determined to forge full steam ahead for my ordination to the priesthood.

With the winds of Vatican II blowing through our midst, everything hitherto unquestioned was now being questioned. Father Mullins, one of the most brilliant minds it has been my privilege to encounter, and others like him were educating us to search for the truth of what it meant to be human and a Christian, in such a way that compelled us to follow the truth no matter where it led. Whereas the realms of the sacred and the secular had previously been totally distinct, the new theological reflection taught that human concerns and human relationships became the disclosure of God, and God came to be in humanity for those whose humanity was open to Him. The great documents of Vatican II, particularly *Gaudium et Spes*, forced us to realise that religious authenticity was always the human authenticity; the two were one, and it was not what we said about God that really mattered, but who we were as a result of our belief in Him.

We were of course conscious of the fact that all around us in Northern Ireland were people, apparently good Christians, dedicated to the destruction of other apparently good Christians who happened not to be of their own denomination. This strengthened our resolve to search for the freedom to be free, to love persons above principles. 'Love one another as I have loved you,' the yardstick of belonging to Jesus Christ, spoke to us in every fibre of our young and idealistic beings.

'*Tu es sacerdos in aeternum*' ('You are a priest for ever') is often printed on the cover of booklets handed out at ordination ceremonies. Each of the four young men being ordained on this day felt quite independently that the vow of celibacy was an unfortunate afterthought, necessarily but unwillingly taken on the road to priesthood, and refused to have '*in aeternum*' printed on our booklets. We understood sexual expression to be part of that incarnate love God had for all people, and it is fair to say that, because we believed in this God and wanted to make His love incarnate for others, we felt deprived, cheated even, of this love in our own lives because of an anachronistic and theologically dubious church law not of our own making. 'Priesthood? Yes! Celibacy? No!' was our cry. Many priests who dare to be honest would say the same.

Small wonder, then, that I felt somewhat castrated as I lay on the cathedral floor before His Lordship the Reverend Doctor Eugene O'Doherty on what was supposed to be the greatest day of my life. My family had hired a minibus to come to Newry for the ordination ceremony, which took place in St Coleman's Cathedral at 10 a.m. on December

20, 1971. Grandparents, parents, sisters and brothers, uncles, aunts, cousins, special friends – all had to come to witness this extraordinary and magnificent event in our family. The proud sighs and sobs of my assembled relatives echoed in my ears as we processed down the aisle, and the Dromantine choir broke into the beautiful and memorable anthem '*Tu es sacerdos in aeternum, sacerdos in aeternum*' (that eternity again!).

In spite of my experience with Alex, I did not – could not – know then that all the theology in the world, all the prayers, masses, communions and rosaries, were no substitute for the love of one human being. We learn to love, not by being told to love, but by being loved; the sun may indeed shine on the just and the unjust alike, as St Matthew would have it, but it shines not on me unless someone touches me.

It seemed churlish to express any of these doubts on my triumphant homecoming to St Michael's Villas. I was the first priest from this side of Ennis ever to be ordained, and the celebrations were unbelievable. I practically had a motorcade of friends and well-wishers from the edge of town to our house. Florry, our resident midwife, childminder and carer for the recently bereaved, had bonfires lit along the neighbourhood streets.

Her full name was Mrs Florry Moroney, but everyone, young and old alike, knew her simply as Florry. She was a big, matronly woman, carrying about nineteen stone, with 'a heart bigger than herself', according to local lore. She was stronger than any man, and woe betide any man who dared cross her. I had given her communion soon after I had been ordained a deacon, when she had been bedridden and housebound. Years later, I wanted to do a doctorate in New York, and my religious order felt unable to pay my fees. Florry offered to bail me out by selling her house and moving into St Joseph's Hospital, formerly the workhouse. Thank goodness, it didn't come to that.

The food was piled high, and the drink flowed. Jack Kelly, our next-door neighbour, had to be helped back to his feet in a glorious state of inebriation after falling on his knees for my blessing. I felt like the Pope.

The following morning the entire town, from the Mayor to the town drunk, turned out to see me celebrate my first holy mass. The primary schools closed down for the day, and the boys from the Christian Brothers' School sang for the service. I spent an interminable amount of time afterwards giving each member of the congregation my blessing, after which my newly consecrated hands would be devoutly kissed.

The mass was followed by a dinner and reception in the Queen's Hotel. After the meal we had the usual speeches. The Mayor, a first cousin of my father's, took it upon himself to give my mother extra special credit for rearing such a good family. Kate, as we affectionately called her, almost literally ascended to heaven. From now on my mother would be referred to as 'the mother of the priest', a title in Irish society superior to royalty and the next best thing to canonisation. The dancing, singing and general merriment lasted into the small hours.

As a newly ordained priest, I was expected to visit – and did so – all the hospitals, nursing homes and other institutions for the sick and disabled, as well as all the schools, primary and secondary, in Ennis, blessing people everywhere I went. I also celebrated a special mass in my father's home village of Clare Castle, followed by another reception at his homestead. Indeed I was wined and dined constantly, though I soon had to cut back on the wining, my tolerance for alcohol being very low in those days. The people of St Michael's Villas made a door-to-door collection and bought me a beautiful transistor radio to take to Africa with me, capable of picking up the BBC World Service.

My most memorable visit was to the railway station, where my father had worked for the last twenty-four years (and from which he has in fact only recently retired). All his workmates gathered to greet me and receive the blessing of the new priest. They presented me with a cheque, money I knew they could ill afford. C. I. E. was not known for its generosity to its employees, and I remembered how when I was a boy my father had not one penny of his week's wages left for himself once he had fed, clothed and educated his family. I knew that these men's children had much the same background as I did; most of them would not see secondary school, let alone dream of a tertiary education. So I felt very much ill at ease when the men knelt before me, for I would always be part of them, yet my new status distanced me.

In this whirlwind of celebrity and celebration, I can truthfully say I was not happy. It was difficult to know where my heart was; wherever it was, it was not my own. I felt, deep within me, a loneliness, a need, which expressed itself most conspicuously through my ever-increasing awareness of my gayness. A lot of my frenetic activity arose out of my need for the acceptance I could not give myself, which in turn only drove me deeper and deeper into alienation. It would be a long time before I realised that it is better to be hated for who you are than to be loved for who you are not. Alienation from self is alienation from God.

I returned to seminary at the beginning of 1972 to complete my theological studies. Ulster was rife with unrest after thirteen young civil rights marchers had been gunned down in Londonderry by the British Army on what came to be known as Bloody Sunday. The next Sunday I joined my fellow students and priests and thousands upon thousands of citizens of Newry on a march to protest against the massacre, the government's intransigence, and the flagrant abuse of Catholic human rights. Although the march was illegal, it went off peacefully.

The six months in seminary gave me a respite from the endless runaround of pre-ordination and ordination. My long years of cloistered study were coming to an end, and I would quite probably never know such peace and security again. Psychologically speaking I was still a child, or at best an adolescent.

I was now supposed to go to Nigeria, but delay followed delay. Alex and I toured Ireland in the summer. In the autumn I studied communications in Dublin, receiving for my labours a certificate in television direction and production. The Secretary of the Institute, on presenting me with my certificate, said, 'Bernard, experience is not everything, but please come back when you have some.'

Chapter
Five

Nothing I had heard, read or been taught in the past seven years had prepared me for Africa, certainly not for the blistering heat of afternoon in the northern Zambian copperbelt. Returning missionaries, visiting African prelates, courses in missiography and missiology – all left me dead to the reality that struck us, a fellow priest from my ordination class and I, when we landed in Ndola. Dressed like Tweedledum and Tweedledee in our missionary-grey clerical suits, we looked like a couple of Mormons plucked from the Tabernacle Choir.

Our final destination was Francisdale, eight miles outside Ndola, the headquarters of our newly founded mission in Zambia. (We were known jocularly as the 'founding fathers'.) We were made most welcome by the other fathers, but I was equally unprepared for the disparity between the living conditions of the missionaries and those of the Africans we were there to serve.

Although we lived poorly, our standard of living was high by comparison. Most of them had no shoes, and owned only the clothes they were wearing. They lived in mud huts, and their staple diet was millet, with the occasional piece of chicken. We had electricity and running water; the majority of the Africans did not. With the naïveté of youth, I determined to do something about it.

My chance came when I was asked to mind the mission house one Sunday afternoon. We had recently received the gift of a television and some carpet from a group of missionary sisters longer established in the country than us. I invited all the local children – a poor, barefooted, raggletaggle bunch – into our newly carpeted television room for a treat. Unfortunately, my superiors returned early, and found me sitting on the floor surrounded by entranced kids, all of us gawping at the box. The brothers took a dim view of having their inner sanctum invaded by these grubby urchins, and I was severely reprimanded, at great cost to my young ego.

This, not surprisingly, made me indignant, believing as I did that our privileged status could only be justified by gestures of this kind, small though they might be. It took me some time to realise that what I had done was not, in my superiors' eyes, 'wrong', in the moral sense; I had simply broken the 'code' by which they all lived. They were decent, respectable men, but they had been brought up in a system of hierarchical privilege in which everything and everybody had a place. I, on the other hand, was a product of the age of the sixties, John XXIII, ecumenism, the vernacular mass and so on. Behaviour like mine could only threaten their way of life, and they did not know how to cope.

Another incident brought this home forcibly. I was staying with the Bishop. He was a good man who had spent all his life in Africa, and had been responsible for the building of many schools, hospitals and churches. One day, after a soccer match, I asked the team captain to join me for a Coca-Cola, and we sat down at the Bishop's dining table. All seemed perfectly natural and in order. But when the bishop came in and found me sitting at his table with a black man, he was dumbfounded. He was not angry, he did not scold or lecture me. He simply could not understand how or why I could do such a thing. Why would anyone want to take someone out of his proper place in the scheme of things? It was all too baffling. You might as well treat young priests with the same respect as bishops, and I wasn't suggesting that, surely?

Indeed not; I knew better than that. I remember a small party given for two Provincial Counsellors who were returning to Ireland after helping to set up the mission. The whisky bottle was produced to wish them a safe journey, and tots were distributed to all; all, that is, except the very youngest priests, who, it was felt, had not reached that point in the social scale where strong drink would be appropriate.

As time passed I came to feel more and more isolated, and that there had to be an alternative way of being a Christian. I had no friend who thought like me, felt like me, questioned like me, laughed like me; nobody seemed to understand me, or be willing to try. I was starved of companionship. Indeed I was so desperate at one point that I had a brief and turbulent affair with a very attractive missionary sister, but this merely compounded my feeling of alienation. I missed my family and friends, but most of all I missed Alex. How I longed for his companionship and understanding!

Finally, after two years in Africa, I plucked up the courage to confide in my local superior about my dissatisfaction. I had learned by this time to be somewhat diplomatic, so I did not go into detail about the conflicts that raged within me. I doubt if he would have understood. So I simply told my superior that in my opinion I was not cut out to stay the course. In spite of my discretion he was anything but sympathetic. After much discussion, not to say argument, it was agreed that I should return to Ireland so that my future could be 'reconsidered'.

My entire family greeted me, in floods of tears, at Shannon Airport. My immediate thought was that my return was not *that* much of a tragedy, and of course I was right. I was shocked and saddened to learn that my nineteen-year-old first cousin, Eric, had been killed on a motorcycle with his friend the previous evening. It was the first of many tragic occasions when I would lead the family in mourning.

I went to see my provincial superior, Father Lawrence Carr, as soon as I could after the funeral. He received me with little cordiality. Father Carr was a man who lived by the book, and applied the book in all his dealings with his subordinates. In his eyes – as he later wrote to a friend of mine – I was a failure, because I 'failed to stay the course as originally contracted'. It was made clear to me that I had only been allowed home so that I could pull myself together, while it was decided what to do with 'this troublesome young priest'.

While they were deliberating they packed me off to Knock, the traditional Marian shrine in County Mayo where the Virgin Mary is believed to have appeared to some farmers. It is regarded as a holy place; to me it seemed like a madhouse. Places like Knock are valuable as places of prayer, but I was sickened by the sexual neuroses displayed by the pilgrims. Devoted husbands and wives, parents of large families, agonised about how to enjoy sex without conception. Women said rosaries and did novenas, substituting holy communion for human communion as their marriages collapsed around them. The real sin, as I saw it, was the way the church persisted in tormenting its own as they confessed to sins which weren't, to my mind, sins at all. If this was the plight of 'normal' heterosexuals, then there wasn't a hope in hell for me. For the first time in my life I contemplated suicide.

During my six-month leave it was tentatively suggested that I should return to Zambia after a year's absence, and stay for three years. I consulted Father Cornelius Murphy at Maynooth, and to him finally, at the age of twenty-six, admitted that I was gay.

Father Murphy advised me to apply to Father Carr for time to pursue extra studies and to sort myself out. It was in fact Father Carr who suggested that I go to Boston. I was to live at the S.M.A. seminary in Dedham, Massachusetts, and take a Master's degree in counselling and psychology at Boston College. It so happened, however, that the Archdiocese of New York needed an associate pastor, and it was decided that I should pursue my studies at Fordham University, at Lincoln Center in New York City. I had a feeling that America would be more to my taste than Africa.

Chapter
Six

My uncle (on my mother's side) met me at Kennedy on August 11, 1975. New York was going through one of its periodic fiscal crises at the time; many of the subways were broken down, and rubbish was piled high in the streets. But this added to my excitement rather than detracted from it. I was drunk with the grandeur of the place; the scream of police cars and sirens had an aphrodisiac effect. I would stand for hours gazing up for a glimpse of the sky between the vertiginous glass walls of the skyscrapers.

I ended up staying with my uncle and his family for a couple of weeks. When I turned up with bags and baggage on the doorstep of Monsignor John Kelly, the man who needed the associate pastor, he looked at me a little askance. After humming and hawing for a while he admitted that he had actually found someone else. 'But don't worry, laddie,' he said brightly. 'We'll put you someplace.'

That 'someplace' eventually turned out to be the parish of St Gabriel's, in the northwest Bronx. Monsignor John A. Carlin, a former army colonel, received me warmly and immediately made me feel at home. Most of what little I owned was still in Africa, since I had left assuming I would be sent back. I didn't even have a clerical shirt or a stock. Monsignor Carlin generously helped me to buy the necessities, and I settled very happily into St Gabriel's. I was to be living in the rectory, celebrating daily mass in the parish, assuming rectory duties two days a week, and pursuing my studies. I was to be paid $50 a month pocket money. There were no language problems, and the food and drink were wholesome and plentiful. Our rooms were cleaned, our beds made, our shoes polished if necessary, our shopping taken care of and our meals cooked. It was all very unlike Africa.

I registered at Fordham and began working for my Master's in the Science of Education Counselling. For a protracted honeymoon period I enjoyed both parish life and university life. The course work was no problem – I maintained an A–B+ average – and fitted in very well with my duties in the parish. I revelled in psychology and avidly read everything I could lay my hands on. I felt inspired as I preached at Sunday mass, bringing psychology and theology together in what I felt was an inevitable marriage. If, I thought, Catholic dogma and doctrine were to be rescued from the mire of their own disembodiment, we had no choice but to make good theology good psychology.

It was a new approach, and as the word got around people began to flock to hear me preach. Indeed, so popular were my sermons that people began calling the rectory to find out when I would next be in the pulpit, since masses rotated each week. This did not go down too well with the other priests in the rectory, but they did their best to be generous about it. I also found the time to write a Catholic syllabus for the sex education of young adults in the grammar school, and soon found that many parishioners, some not so young either, came to seek my advice on matters both psychological and spiritual. My ego had never been so gratified, and I loved it. For the first time, I felt I was being used to my full human potential.

In my own classes at Fordham I was challenged by my peers in group therapy – a prerequisite for my degree course. At the same time, at the instigation of my mentor Father

Hennessy, I started personal psychoanalysis, which I found both traumatic and tremendously useful. I was, to coin a phrase, going places in my inner life, and delighted with this newfound growth.

I could not and did not say I was gay. In class I became the object of the affections of two particularly attractive young women. While, as always, I enjoyed the attention, I dared not become involved, not just for their sake but for mine as well. In my experience many women are attracted to priests – a safe haven, if you like – and I see no particular harm in it. On the whole, women with whom I have become involved have respected the vow of celibacy, and accept that there is no prospect of a sexual relationship. Even so, I found that if I concealed my gayness, which I had to, the demands of the relationship very quickly progressed to a point where I felt uncomfortable. As usual, I took no pleasure in being gay; my guilt about my desires and fantasies was the only blot on the horizon.

In the summer of 1977 I was awarded my MSc degree in counselling. Since the occasion was primarily a family day, I did not attend the graduation ceremony. I was therefore spared having to witness something else that happened that day, something that was ultimately to change my whole life. I heard about it the next morning: a fellow graduate had thrown himself twenty-six floors from our classroom window into the plaza at Lincoln Center. I was numb with shock. I had known Jimmy well – we had often exchanged class notes in the university library, particularly when examinations were coming up. I knew he had a drinking problem, but I had no idea that he was in such dreadful pain. I called his parish, which was next to mine in the Bronx, and requested permission to celebrate Jimmy's funeral Mass the next morning. Monsignor John Doherty kindly granted my wish.

As I came out of the church after the requiem, I noticed a small group of people standing apart from the rest of the mourners. Partly out of curiosity and partly out of instinct, I approached them, assuming (correctly) that they were friends of Jimmy's. They turned out to be members of an organisation for Catholic lesbians and gays called Dignity. I was stunned, because I had no idea that Jimmy was gay.

The man who seemed to be their spokesman, Andy Humm, asked if I would celebrate mass for them.

'Of course,' I said. And why not? Celebrating mass was, after all, a large part of my job. Up to now I had had no contact with gay people in New York, and knew nothing of any organisation like Dignity. I was pleased and flattered that they had asked *me* to be their celebrant. Perhaps I already sensed that their destiny and mine were already linked. I was taken aback when I discovered that Dignity were forced to celebrate mass in a rented Protestant church – the Church of the Good Shepherd, behind Lincoln Center – because the Archdiocese had refused to allow them to use a Catholic church.

I was now twenty-eight years old. Gradually at first, and then with greater intensity, I took on the role of leader of this beleaguered community. It was a role that both excited and alarmed me. It may seem odd that I still had not openly admitted that I was gay, but so oppressive is the homophobia that gay people suffer that it can take a lifetime to come out of the closet.

Among the sixty or so in the congregation that first night I celebrated was a young Capuchin friar of German-Irish extraction, who appeared to me the absolute epitome of psychic health and self-acceptance. We became close friends, and he was vital to my becoming adult about my sexual orientation. He was perfectly comfortable about being gay and a priest. 'That's the Church's problem,' he would say. To my surprise, admitting my sexuality to myself (and to myself only) felt as though a great weight had been lifted off my shoulders. It was a momentous admission.

Father John McNeil had just published, after much hassle from the church authorities, his pioneering book *The Church and the Homosexual.* (As a result of publishing the book he was silenced by the Vatican; after ten years he broke the silence and was consequently suspended from the Jesuits.) We in Dignity were much influenced by his work, and through the mediation of some important friends in high places, were invited by the pastor of a Jesuit parish, St Francis Xavier in Greenwich Village, to come and worship in their beautiful old Gothic church. There was much joy and celebration amongst our community at finding our own home, and after this momentous move our numbers doubled, trebled and quadrupled. Soon we were packing upwards of six hundred gay and lesbian people into Saturday evening mass. I was elected to the Dignity Board of Directors alongside a fellow priest, the Reverend Bob Carter SJ.

Having completed my Master's degree, I was anxious to continue my studies and get my Doctorate; I felt that I had really only scratched the surface, as it were, both academically and personally. I had a battle of words with my superiors in Ireland, and for over a year there was an unholy silence between us. Then the Vice-Provincial wrote to say that he was sending me a one-way ticket to Ireland, but threats never work with me, and I very politely told him what to do with it. At last, after much ado, it was decided by my superiors in Ireland that I would be left alone to pursue doctoral studies if I paid my own way. So I had to get a job.

I drew up my resumé and applied for positions at various schools and colleges in the New York area. When Mount St Michael's Academy offered me the post of teacher of religious knowledge I was delighted to accept, since it gave me both the free time and the money to study, with enough left over for a studio apartment in the Bronx.

Mount St Michael's, owned and operated by the Catholic Marist Brothers, is a highly respected private high school with an excellent academic track record. Founded in 1926 with a registration of sixty-two boys, by the time I went there in

1978 it had a complement of 1200 pupils and seventy-one staff, forty of them lay. The students were a far cry from the meek, obedient Irish lads of my day; many of them came from broken or violent homes. Although I had been hired as a teacher, I soon moved on to founding a campus ministry, the first such on the campus in twenty years. The students sought me out for advice on every conceivable problem, from the regular 'I don't believe in God any more', to the astonishing (to me, at any rate) 'Father, my girlfriend is pregnant, can you loan me the money for an abortion?'. There were even problems with the occasional boy acting as a male hustler, with furtive and guilt-ridden encounters with prostitutes, and so on.

My office, or 'Padré's hangout' as it became known, was wonderful, with huge cushions on the floor and posters all over the walls. As the boys came to trust me it became a haven for them. I was the closest thing to a father many of them had ever known, and in a sense they were 'my' children. I would plead with their mothers to take them back after they had been thrown out. The police would occasionally call and ask me to pick them up from street corners or precinct houses when they got into trouble. I went to the hospital with some of them when they overdosed and had to be rushed to the emergency room to have their stomachs pumped. It was not unusual for me to find one of my students waiting on my doorstep when I got home at night, because he had nowhere else to go.

I was to be chaplain at Mount St Michael's for six years, running what the church authorities regarded – and reported – as a 'model campus ministry'. I shared my clothes and food with the boys. I gave them all the love I had, and they returned it a hundredfold. I had never been happier.

Meanwhile, I continued my studies, for which Mount St Michael's gave me Mondays free. I was working towards a Doctorate in Ministry – an interdisciplinary degree in psychology and theology – at New York Theological Seminary, which was actually a Protestant institution. The competing needs of everything I was involved in meant that I rarely had more than three or four hours sleep a night, but I revelled in my workaholism. Each part of my life complemented the others perfectly, and I felt very fulfilled.

I was taking a more prominent role in Dignity, and was devoting at least one night a week to the gay Catholic community. We had started a gay clergy support group, which met once a month in the apartment of one of the members. There were now between twenty and thirty of us priests meeting regularly and serving the needs of the gay and lesbian community. There was no open conflict with the church at this point, although from the beginning Dignity had felt the force of official disapproval of special masses for gay and lesbian people, on the grounds that 'their needs, like other special interest groups', should be taken care of within the ordinary parish structure'. It became clear that the Jesuits of St Francis Xavier were on the Chancery hitlist, so it was not altogether a surprise when Dignity were finally expelled from 'Church property' in November 1986.

The first inkling I got that *I* had incurred the wrath of the Archdiocesan authorities was when my provincial superior in Cork received a complaint from the Chancellor of the Archdiocese that I had been a delegate to the Dignity International Convention in Philadelphia. In particular, Bishop O'Keefe's objection was that 'Father Lynch believes that gay is good'. My Provincial was perturbed, but not excessively so. He pressed the Chancery for clarification: to what, precisely, from the point of view of dogma and doctrine, were the authorities objecting? After all, I was entitled to my opinion, was I not? No reply was ever forthcoming, and for the moment things were on hold.

Chapter
Seven

The first to die was Gustavo from Colombia. He committed suicide in 1981 because he thought he had contracted the disease with no name. The terrible illness struck the community without warning; suddenly, with horrible regularity, friends were getting sick and dying. Today, of the six hundred or so PWAs to whom I have ministered, only six are still alive. After our Saturday-night liturgies at St Xavier's, more and more people were talking about friends who had contracted this mysterious illness. Father Declan was missing his words at his Palm Sunday mass, and couldn't see clearly; by Friday week he was dead. Increasingly the prayers of the faithful during mass became a litany for the sick with their horrific symptoms: swollen lymph nodes, pneumonia, diarrhoea, coughing, thrush, tiredness and inertia, Kaposi's sarcoma, showing purple spots on the skin, and on and on. Almost every day someone died, and the medical profession had little idea why. It wasn't long, of course, before the media christened it 'the gay plague'.

As a priest I was spending more and more of my time visiting the sick, anointing the dying, officiating at funerals, and finding my duties emotionally and physically draining. Like everyone else, I lived in hope, but it just went on and on. There were no tests, no drugs, no cure; you got sick and you died. The *New York Native*, a gay paper, came up with what we thought at the time was a sensationalist headline: 1200 AND STILL COUNTING. The search for scapegoats began, as if people could protect themselves by constructing theories: only the very promiscuous got it, the ones who went in for a lot of anal or oral sex; only those who took drugs; only those who had been injected against hepatitis-B, or who had had syphilis or African swine fever; only those who used poppers. But we all knew in our hearts that anyone could get it, though none of us wanted to condemn ourselves to death by admitting it. And all the time people were dying, dying, dying, and still asking, 'Why me, why me?'

While I was dealing as best I could with all the suffering that surrounded me, another crisis arose. Back in 1978 Father Jeremy Mullins, the priest in whom I had confided my relationship with Alex, had called me from London to ask for my help with something that had been troubling him. Despite the fact that I was now a priest myself I still held him in considerable awe – he was still my hero, and one of the greatest priests I had ever known. We met in Ireland, and although he was guarded in his manner, it was obvious he was undergoing tremendous conflicts about his priesthood. Soon afterwards he came to New York, and to my amazement admitted that he, too, was having problems with his sexuality; had, indeed, been struggling with it at the time he had counselled me. He told me how he had both envied and loathed the experience I had described.

My immediate reaction was that Jeremy had to get into therapy, and with someone who understood both sexuality and the priesthood. A friend, Father John Lee, recommended Father Jim Cotter, an Anglo-Catholic in London who over the next three years or so tried his best to put Jeremy's tortured soul back together again.

Jeremy and I spent Christmas of 1978 in San Francisco. He loved it, and wanted to settle there immediately. He and I had moved from a professor and confessor/student relationship to one of easy friendship. I admired and respected his brilliance, his great insight into human nature, and above all else his compassion. He could see worth in everyone except, sadly, himself. He was unhappy, terribly unhappy, and no amount of meetings between us – and there were four in all between 1978 and 1981, including a six-month sabbatical I spent with him in London – could satisfy the need he felt to live a life free of parental control, as he saw his relationship with the Church. As usual our Provincial was both sympathetic and supportive. We agreed that Jeremy's request for laicisation ought not to be approved at this point, because we felt that he was not sure enough of himself to take such an extreme position. Instead he was granted leave of absence, which meant that, although he did not have a licence to perform any of the priestly functions, he was still a priest.

Jeremy arrived in New York City in the summer of 1981, his possessions few and his finances meagre. I moved out of my studio at 3065 Broadway, leaving him the furnishings and paying the rent for three months, so that he could have a start. I moved to a small apartment in Riverdale, in the Bronx, which I furnished with the help of friends. (The previous spring I had started practising psychotherapy privately two evenings a week in order to supplement my income, and so I was not only willing but able to help my friend.) Brother Ryan, principal of Mount St Michael's, agreed to employ Jeremy as a counsellor, even though his immigration status was, for the time being, unclear.

For the first time in his life, at the ripe old age of forty-four, Jeremy was having to make his way in the real world, to cook and clean, do the laundry and pay the bills. Many clergy find it immensely difficult to adjust after a lifetime of privilege in their closed society, and Jeremy was no exception. (I had been out on my own since 1977, so I had acquired a certain ease in dealing with what most people take for granted.) Jeremy joined Dignity and threw himself into Greenwich Village life with enthusiasm.

*　　*　　*

In September 1982 my mother died suddenly at the tragically early age of fifty-nine. Because I had had such a good relationship with her, especially in the later years of her life, I was able to accept her death with a certain amount of equanimity, although the fact that it signalled the end of my Irish home life saddened me. She, like my father, had been highly supportive of my gay identity, and I still cherish the loving letter of acceptance she wrote me after I 'came out'. She was a deeply religious woman, though not the sainted Irish mother for whom religion was a sad and life-denying thing; for her, religion was life-affirming and liberating. Hers was a loving God who knew the tears, a Mother God in every sense of the word. As the marvellous English mystic Julian of Norwich put it, 'As truly as God is our father, so truly is God our mother.' Her life taught me that time is on the side of those who love, and yet how little there is for any of us. There is so much to be done, so many need our light, but I cannot promise myself tomorrow, only today. Only today have I a life to live and with which to love. This truth was indelibly marked on my soul with the death of my mother.

The Church authorities, meanwhile, were running scared, and with Father Declan's passing the grim reaper seemed very close. Jeremy, like the rest of us, was one of the 'worried, well and anxious', but still of the mind that the sick and dying must have been into some unusual and dangerous form of homosexual activity. Then in the spring of 1983 Jeremy complained that he was not feeling too well. Seeing that he was unhappy in his work at school and that his salary never seemed to be enough to keep him going, we both assumed that his circumstances were getting him down. We concluded that he was inevitably somewhat depressed, and that he ought to see his therapist, Father Bob Carter SJ, more often, which he did.

Jeremy decided to leave Mount St Michael's in the summer and re-enter the Society of African Missions, taking up an opportunity which had come up at our seminary in Dedham, Mass. For a man of his brilliance, education and experience, he was under-used and under-appreciated at the Academy. The new principal, Paul Daigneault, the first layman to hold the post, was unsympathetic to Jeremy's mental state, and more than once tried to force the issue of his laicisation. I believed that this was none of his business, and indeed Daigneault himself, as a former Christian Brother, was not exactly an objective outsider on the issue. By the time he left Mount St Michael's Jeremy was seriously ill, losing weight and suffering from serious fatigue and inertia. We didn't discuss his condition much, and continued to ignore the evidence of our own eyes. We hoped that a change of scene and job would bring back the old Jeremy. He couldn't possibly have AIDS, I told myself.

When I returned from my summer vacation in Ireland Jeremy had moved to Boston. I wanted to visit him, but he insisted that he was missing New York and his friends there, and in any case he wanted to see his psychotherapist. When I met him at LaGuardia airport I couldn't believe my eyes; he had lost so much weight. But he insisted he was feeling fine. We drove to the beach, and had a terrific day swimming, sunbathing and chatting about everything and everyone under the sun. Jeremy was in good spirits, and as usual we engaged in some heavy theology, discussing the afterlife, the existence of God and Jesus, the meaning of the Church. This was to be the last such conversation I would have with my great mentor; in retrospect I think he had some idea of what was going to happen. He argued, strangely on the defensive, for an afterlife, while I played the devil's advocate, trying to burst every theological bubble he could come up with as a reason to believe.

The following day Jeremy was too ill to make it to his appointment with Father Carter, and he had to take a cab the quarter of a mile back to the apartment from the subway. When I saw him off to Boston he kept assuring and reassuring me that he would be all right, it was only a matter of time before he was better. I was desperate to believe him. The alternative, that my spiritual father had AIDS, was too awful to contemplate.

Two weeks later he went into Boston General Medical Center for tests; the diagnosis was lymphoma, cancerous but apparently treatable with chemotherapy. At last we had found the cause of his physical deterioration. When I flew up to see him in October he was in good spirits, convinced that the chemotherapy was working. He certainly looked no worse than he had in August, so I was happy to go along with his mood. I thought it better not to probe. By the end of October he was back in hospital, and between then and Christmas I shuttled back and forth every other weekend to see my dear friend.

On one such occasion I met Jeremy's brother from Texas, Bruce, who was also a priest, although not one with Jeremy's special qualities. Jeremy had never had much time for him; they differed in everything – sexual orientation, theology and church politics – and were very different personalities. I found Father Bruce a rather ordinary man, with none of Jeremy's intellectual brilliance or sense of humour, just like many a priest back home in Ireland. He and I got on well enough, though, and I had no premonition of the madness that lay ahead.

Jeremy spent Christmas in Texas with his brother. When I called in the New Year I discovered that he was back in hospital. I immediately called the hospital and reached Bruce, who told me that this was a bad time to speak and that I should call him at his rectory the following morning. There was no answer when I did so, and the hospital told me that no calls were being put through to Jeremy's room. Despite many attempts over the next couple of days I failed to reach either Jeremy or Bruce; I had to be content with leaving messages that I was concerned for my friend, and that I was ready to fly down if necessary.

I was in my office at Mount St Michael's when Bruce finally called. I was terrified that he was about to tell me

Jeremy was dead, and did my best to prepare myself. What I actually heard was the most astonishing, unjust and painful tirade; the man sounded demented. 'You are not to call here,' he screamed. 'You are not to visit. You will be evicted by the police if you come near here. My brother is dying and you are to stay away. I will tell everything I know about you to your family and your order. He's asked to see you but I've told him you are in Ireland, and that's all he's going to know. Remember, I will make trouble for you if you try to call or visit my brother. And in the event of his death you are not to come to his funeral, you are to stay away. I will tell everything.'

I put down the receiver, dumbfounded. I simply could not understand the venom of this priest, this so-called representative of Christ. I had been Jeremy's friend, and he had been mine; he was asking for me on his deathbed, yet his own brother took it upon himself to deny his wish. I had to accept that Bruce was grieving for his brother, but his behaviour was not only unchristian but downright cruel.

I was still smarting the next day when the school secretary asked me to come to her office urgently. She handed me a letter to the school principal from Father Bruce, making the most outrageous allegations. I immediately showed the letter to the principal, and called my Provincial in Ireland to inform him of the contents. I was advised to do and say nothing. I obeyed, painful though it was.

Jeremy died on January 17, 1984, at the age of 47. It was his sister who called from London to tell me that he was to be buried in Ireland. I was of course forbidden to attend. It was not until Easter that I heard for sure (from the Vice-Provincial at the S.M.A. headquarters in New Jersey) that Jeremy had died of AIDS. Bruce, it seemed, blamed me not only for his brother's death but for his very homosexuality as well.

I tried as best I could to continue my work, at Mount St Michael's, with Dignity, and as a psychotherapist. With my dear friend now dead and buried I thought that, at least, I would be rid of his brother and his vile accusations. I couldn't have been more wrong. He continued to pester me and my friends with hate mail, accusing me, among other things, of having stolen Jeremy's personal effects. At first I simply ignored the letters, hoping he would get tired of badgering me if there was no reaction. But eventually I was forced to hire an attorney to rebut his accusations and prove to him that Jeremy had given what few things he owned to some friends; I had nothing. It is an indication of Father Bruce's sorry state that he tracked down the gay couple in question through Jeremy's address book and denounced them to their employers – on church stationery.

Jeremy's death and his brother's craziness are what breached the wall. I felt I was going to be next. It was so hard to keep a sense of proportion – I felt I had lived a whole life in AIDS. But trouble was looming from another quarter altogether.

Chapter
Eight

The late spring of 1984 was a momentous time for New York's gay community. The press and television were full of the Mayor's Executive Order #50, which forbade discrimination against gays or lesbians from employers who did business with the city or received city funding. All this legislation was intended to do was to guarantee people – taxpaying citizens of a different sexual orientation – equal opportunity; in other words, the taxes they paid were not to be used to discriminate against them in employment. It was an important and courageous step towards protecting the rights of a minority group. The Salvation Army, and the Catholic Church of the Archdiocese of New York, under the new leadership of Archbishop O'Connor (he had not yet been made a cardinal), opposed the legislation vehemently.

Each year on the last Sunday in June Dignity, with scores of other religious and secular groups, marched in a parade – second in size only to St Patrick's Day – to celebrate gay and lesbian pride. In 1984 I was elected by the Board to lead the prayers on the steps of St Patrick's Cathedral. The practice had been for some years to conclude with a recitation of the 'Our Father' while holding hands. That year was no exception, but as I descended the cathedral steps I suddenly found myself surrounded by a crowd of press reporters and television cameras. A microphone was shoved into my face and I was asked, out of the blue, 'Father, what do you think of the Archbishop's objection to the executive order?' It was, in fact, quite a normal question to be asked. I had earned a small reputation as being active in securing human rights wherever possible, so naturally enough the press would be curious about how I would react to an Archbishop who apparently gave not one whit for the rights of some members of the Catholic flock. I answered simply by saying, 'Employment is a basic human right for *all* people – men, women, black, white, gay and heterosexual.' That seemed to me to be a proper and not at all controversial statement.

By that evening, however, my statement had been transformed into something rather different. One headline had it, PRIEST OPPOSES ARCHBISHOP; another, ARCHBISHOP DOES NOT BELIEVE IN BASIC HUMAN RIGHTS CLAIMS PRIEST. It would, of course, have blown over by the next day had not the Archbishop decided to reiterate his opposition, stating in the *New York Post* that he would 'close all my orphanages rather than employ one gay person'. This was a particularly vile statement, since by using the orphanages as an example the Archbishop may have left the impression that gayness was to be equated with child molestation – something that was anathema to everyone, gay and heterosexual alike.

I was warned by friends that I was heading for an all-out confrontation with the Archbishop, and at that time I did not want any such thing. The Archbishop was my superior and I felt it would be wrong to drag both him and the Church into the headlines any further. I had some holidays due, so I decided to go to Ireland and let things cool down.

On my return to New York and to Mount St Michael's the principal, Mr Daigneault, told me that he had received several calls from the Chancery demanding my resignation. He also told me that he had referred the matter to the Marist Provincial and his council who, in turn, would be in touch with my Provincial and council in Ireland. My Provincial responded to both Bishop O'Keefe and to the Marist Provincial that in his view my support for gay and lesbian people in their struggle for civil rights was in no way dissident to Church dogma or doctrine vis-à-vis homosexuality. Only after I undertook that as long as I worked at Mount St Michael's I would not make my involvement with Dignity a 'media issue' did the principal agree to let the matter rest, however uneasily. The Archdiocese, however, would not accept this. They wanted me out at all costs. But the school refused, saying I was a good priest and that my work at the school was excellent and my behaviour irreproachable. They also pointed out that they had been asking the Archdiocese for a priest for twenty years before my arrival but with no success.

I was showering after my daily run when I was told that the principal wanted to see me pronto. When I got to his office he handed me an envelope, saying simply, 'You'd better see this.' It contained a copy of the letter Jeremy's brother had written in June along with a selection of anti-homosexual literature that was, for the most part, either salacious or pornographic. It appeared that Father Bruce had been seen outside the school, in full clerical garb, distributing this material to the students as they made their way home, and placing it on the windshields of teachers' cars. I was shattered. I instantly contacted my Provincial, took legal advice, and had counsel from the Marist Provincial. All agreed, for the hundredth time, that the wise thing to do was to 'sit tight and do nothing', and above all to keep the matter from the media. Three times in the next six weeks Father Bruce picketed the school with a placard that read, FATHER LYNCH — PERVERT. DO YOU WANT HIM NEAR YOUR SONS?

A faculty meeting was called asking for my resignation (after one of the teachers met with Father Bruce), but seventy-three of the seventy-eight teachers voted in my support, and they forwarded a signed petition to the principal and administration requesting that my resignation neither be requested, nor accepted should I volunteer it.

I felt vindicated. Unknown to me, however, the three

51

teachers who had called the faculty meeting to demand my resignation had had telephone contact with Father Bruce in Texas.

Two weeks later to the day, and again two weeks after that, Father Bruce appeared outside the school, always in full clerical regalia, bearing his infamous placard. The principal was still under pressure from the Archdiocese to get rid of me. The school was in turmoil, but I am proud to say that not one student or parent made a complaint against me or issued a demand that I resign. There were meetings and counter-meetings between faculty and administration. The school was suffering; more importantly, as far as I was concerned, so were the students. I realised that I could not continue in such an untenable position. So, having lost the support of the principal, and being continually targeted by the crazy Father Bruce, I resigned my position as campus minister at Mount St Michael's on December 20, 1984.

When things go wrong, and the good Lord knows they can go very wrong, one can find oneself in troubles so deep and so bizarre that one knows one can never get out of them, and it doesn't help at all to recognise that much of one's trouble is produced by the unreadable and unpredictable convolutions of one's own character. I sat sometimes really helpless and terrified before my own life, watching it spread danger and wonder all over my landscape, and not only my own. It is a terrible feeling. One learns at such moments not merely how little we know but how little whatever we know is able to help us.

The only thing that kept me sane during all this was the perhaps naïve conviction that since I had done nothing wrong, no wrong would happen to me. Of course there is evil in the world, but I could not make myself believe that even Father Bruce in his vitriolic anger was anything but deranged. Dangerous, yes, but surely not deliberately evil. I also saw myself caught up in a situation not all of my own making. With the upsurge of AIDS in the gay community I was pitched into a continuous encounter with death. In a sense I had to die myself in order to be able to go through the searing task of comforting others on that most solitary and frightening journey. I accepted, although I did not always understand, that the Love of God was my ultimate environment, and that in believing this, then I would live, regardless of the cost. While in my preaching and teaching I exhorted people to the ideals of Christian chastity in pastoral practice, I always strove to accept people for what they were. My attitude to Father Bruce was no different.

Meanwhile, having founded the Dignity AIDS ministry earlier in the year, I became more and more involved in home, hospital and street ministry. I increased my private psychotherapy practice, and became a member of the Mayor's task force on AIDS.

With the increase in AIDS cases reaching epidemic proportions in 1986, the need to introduce legislation to protect gay and lesbian people in their civil rights to housing and employment became paramount. It was unfortunate, though expected, that the Church adamantly came out against legislation: the city's Catholic gay community was infuriated by the continuous stream of homophobic statements that flowed from the Chancery of the New York Archdiocese. We were burying more and more people, yet certain Archdiocesan priests were refusing to celebrate masses for the dead, or to take funeral services.

In March 1986, Bishop Paul Moore, the Episcopal bishop of the diocese of New York, asked if someone from the Catholic community would join him, Rabbi Balfour Brickner and the Reverend Dr Sloan Coffin of Riverside Church in issuing a public statement in support of the civil rights of the gay and lesbian community. Bishop Sullivan, the Catholic co-adjutor bishop of Brooklyn Diocese, was to have done this task but allegedly was forbidden to do so by the Cardinal Archbishop. The political leadership of New York asked for and received every help from the Dignity leadership in its counter-offensive to the politicking of the archdiocese. The Brooklyn diocese was open at first, and under Bishop

Sullivan drew up an alternative document in the hope of appeasing the Church. But it was to no avail. Needless to say tempers flared as, once again, the gay community witnessed itself being sacrificed in the name of Christ.

On March 20, 1986, New York City, for the first time in its history, passed legislation guaranteeing lesbian and gay New Yorkers work and housing without prejudice to their sexual orientation.

I had been called to testify at the hearings, and it is an indication of how dangerous the Church had made the situation that after the hearing I had to receive an armed police escort from the Chambers to the subway as Catholic right-wing groups, together with Hassidic Jews and others, chanted, 'Shame, shame, put him on the plane.'

When I first entered the Chambers the security guard automatically assumed I was there 'for the Cardinal', since I wore my religious garb, and placed me among the religious 'right': the Knights of Columbus, the Holy Name Society, the Hassidic and Orthodox Jews. And when I got up to speak all these assumed I would support the discrimination my Church seemed determined to promulgate. I introduced myself as an S.M.A. Father, and continued by saying that having lived and, indeed, having been ordained in Northern Ireland, I knew what discrimination was all about. The right-wingers applauded. The gay community were silent. I then added, 'I am here today to give my wholehearted support to the just and legitimate gospel rights of lesbian and gay people to be protected against discrimination in matters of accommodation and of employment, and I see this as absolutely consistent with the social justice claimed by Jesus Christ, when He said, "As often as you did this to the least, you did it to Me."'

As I came off the set of the Phil Donahue talk show in March 1986 – St Patrick's Day, in fact – a man approached me. He said to me, quite aggressively, 'We are going to find a boy to accuse you.' He was a member of one of those right-wing groups of Catholics, highly articulate and far more dangerous than I ever realised. I shrugged and said, 'Okay, do,' and really thought no more of it.

After the jubilation of the passage of the gay rights bill had subsided, it was back to business as usual, and the awful, grinding struggle to fight AIDS: assisting those who were ill, caring for the dying, and enabling those who suffered from opportunistic infections to secure their just and legitimate rights in the city.

People were angry at the Church and the State for doing so little so late. The politicians were, as they say, 'straining a gnat and swallowing a camel' in order to keep the powermongers of the church and state happy while those with AIDS died without having their most fundamental rights met.

In those days – only a few years ago – it was not unusual to go to the hospital and find AIDS patients' meals left stone cold at their doors since the orderlies were afraid they would catch the disease if they went into the rooms. Funeral homes refused to take the corpses of those who had died with AIDS. More than once we were forced to carry friends from hospitals in bodybags in search of some sympathetic funeral parlour because no one else would touch them.

It was a terrible time. Parents and families of sufferers did not want to know their sons were gay and dying of the so-called 'gay plague'. More ashes of PWAs have gone into the Hudson River at the end of Christopher Street, Pier 42, than I care to recall.

Then, in the autumn of 1986, the Vatican issued its infamous letter on the pastoral care of homosexual people. In this letter gay people were labelled as 'disordered in their nature and evil in their love' and those of us who supported the human and civil rights of such people were 'not to be surprised when violence was visited on you'.

The reaction in the city and throughout the gay world – and, indeed, among many other reasonable, intelligent people – was incredulity. How could the Church, a Church supposedly based on the love of humankind, issue such a horrendously offensive document? We were devastated. I supported Reverend John McNeill, who took a public stand against the letter. He was suspended from his order after forty years of caring service in the Jesuits. I was blackballed by the Cardinal Archbishop. He refused me canonical faculties in the archdiocese of New York, by which action he made it virtually impossible for me to work as a priest anywhere in the United States. In short, he saw to it that I was unemployable.

As a way out of this impasse my superiors ordered me in June 1987 to take a sabbatical in Rome in order, as they delicately put it, to 'recuperate'. My reputation, however, had gone before me, and I was a kind of pariah in the community. I was being forced into making a choice: either to go mad, or to go outside the community and join those people who risked involvement with others as the only guarantee of any eternity. I stayed at the Generalate, where my confrères were nice, but there was little empathy for the cause of sexual minorities. There was a gay community in the city, but there were also many living double lives: married, with hidden gay relationships. I quietly buried ashes of gay friends from San Francisco at Assisi, attended university, and was invited to lecture in London later in the year.

I had been in Rome a month when a TV documentary about myself and my ministry, called 'AIDS – A Priest's Testament', was transmitted on both Irish Television and Channel 4 in Britain. I went to Dublin for the occasion, and used the publicity surrounding it to further the cause of people with AIDS. I truly did not realise that this would make me even more of a target for the fanatics determined to see me brought to heel.

By Christmas I was longing to return to my work in New York. However, it was made clear in the New Year that if I wanted to remain a member of the Society of African Missions I would have to sign a document drawn up by the Congregation of Religious, promising to be faithful to Church teaching in matters of faith and morals. I did sign, but this did not pacify the Archdiocese, nor did it clear the way for my fulltime return to New York. I waited and waited in Europe for word. Nothing arrived, so I went on retreat for eight days, under the direction of Jesuit Father Michael Paul Gallagher, then teaching at University College Dublin. I decided to return to New York without institutional church support; having cleared this with my provincial superior, I booked my ticket. Within twenty-four hours of making the booking I heard from a priest friend in London that the FBI was looking for me. I was to be indicted on a charge of sexual abuse in the first degree, arising out of accusations made by a fourteen-year-old Mount St Michael's student called John Schaefer.

PART II

A PRIEST ON TRIAL

Chapter
Nine

Nobody who has not been on the receiving end of media attention can really imagine what it is like. The press camped on my father's doorstep in Ennis, County Clare, and tortured him day and night with phone calls. My father had always been a very private man, so this unwelcome attention hit him very hard. They also besieged my Provincial's house at Blackrock Road, Cork, calling him up constantly for an interview or to make some comment. He handled the situation with great integrity despite his genuine nervousness around the complexities of the issues. He was the first to say publicly that I had been accused only, not yet tried and convicted, as the media were already making out.

It was decided that I should hire a lawyer to defend me in court, although we all still hoped against hope that it would not come to this. My friends in New York were marvellous. They spoke to other lawyers, to friendly contacts in the Bronx District Attorney's office, and decided to launch a media counter-attack by calling a press conference of their own, under the leadership of a prominent AIDS activist and writer, Charles Frederick. Many felt that this was a witch-hunt and that the Archdiocese was out to make an example of me. This appalled many in my community, and so priest and nun friends, people with AIDS, former parishioners, Dignity sisters and brothers, all gathered at the Gay Community Centre on 13th Street in Greenwich Village, and aired their views to television and press. Their action was a great comfort, but my heart did not understand what was happening to me, even though I could understand and know clearly with my mind.

I turned to the greatest comfort any priest can have – prayer. I have always prayed, reflected, listened with joy to sacred music in the presence of God. I have done this not from any sense of duty or obligation, but out of that inner space in me that sought to be in touch with the mystery of life. The real purpose of my prayer was that through it I came to understand the questions I was asking of God; I learned to live with the lack of answers, always receiving a greater sense of my centredness. Jesus, for me, was the measure of what it meant for me to be in God. In Jesus I found the way to see that life was not absurd and meaningless, but gracious, forgiving and grounded in love. And so the love of God was and is for me my ultimate environment, what I am made from and what I am made for. I absolutely believe, even though I do not always understand, that God's love is not simply what ought to be, but what is, and out of that reality I live and move and have my being.

Small wonder, then, that when I found myself caught in this labyrinth of political intrigue I prayed harder than I had ever done. I prayed to God, to St Martin de Porres, to St Thérèse of Lisieux, beseeching them to work some kind of miracle and halt this monstrous charade. They didn't. They had other plans, and ever so slowly I accepted God's will in this as being for my good.

Before I returned to New York and handed myself over to the FBI, I was questioned by Mr Patrick McAntee, the barrister hired by my religious order to initiate my defence, in Dublin. He didn't pull any punches. His first question was, 'Are you gay?'

'Yes, sir.'

'You denied so being on the *Late, Late Show*.'

'Yes. I did. But I believed it was the right thing to do at the time.'

'Well, it wasn't.'

'I know that now.'

'Do you believe in Jesus Christ?'

'Yes. And I believe in His gospel message of liberating love for all people, and especially my own. These are my people, gays and lesbians, PWAs.'

'Why do you believe this?'

'It's what Jesus taught.'

'Huh. You're one of the few priests I know who believes that. And you know what happened to Jesus, I suppose? Now then, you come here in tears and shock and dismay, asking for help for what has happened to you. Let's see what we can do.'

It was unbelievably painful to have to go over time and time again the details of my accuser's visit to my apartment on that evening of January 1986. I could not deny that he had indeed been there, nor did I wish to. But that I had attempted to seduce him was simply not what happened. I specifically requested that both my Provincial and his Vice-Provincial be present at the interviews in Dublin. I did this partly for moral support but mostly because, given the hideous nature of the press coverage in Ireland, I was beginning, for the first time, to doubt my innocence in my own soul. Self-love and self-hate, like all forms of love and hate, are very close, and I was at the brink. I knew that I must keep faith, that I must transform my sorrow into life, but it was very difficult.

The next several weeks were spent trying to arrange my safe return to New York. Father Laurence and my friends Conor and Roísin McAnally provided a safe house for me between Dublin and Cork where I could escape the hounding of the media. It is one of the great tragedies of this whole awful affair that nowhere was I to be more of a target for hatred than in the Irish press. They printed eye-catching exaggerations, misquotations and imaginative stories without ever checking the facts, and seemingly without a care in the world that they were causing irreparable damage to me, my dear father, my family and religious community. The *Star* ran a front-page headline with a picture of my bewildered father. MY SON IS NO MONSTER, it read, although my father told me he had never spoken to them. Even the so-called 'respectable' newspapers – the *Irish Press*, the *Irish Independent*, the *Cork Examiner* – showed a marked lack of integrity. The *Irish Times* and the *Sunday Tribune* were the only exceptions. The *Times* carried a statement of the *facts* from my Provincial, while the *Tribune* was the first to check out the truth of the indictment and print that it was *one* boy making the accusation and not *several* as the other papers claimed.

I reached rock-bottom one day when I was in a pub in Dublin called 'The Old Stand' with a fellow S.M.A. student who was commiserating with me over a pint. I noticed two men staring at me, and remarked on this to my friend, admitting that I could be paranoid. When my friend went to the bar to get another drink the two men approached me and one of them threw his beer in my face while the other shouted, 'Pervert! You've destroyed the good name of Mount St Michael's. You fucking faggot!'

I was quite literally paralysed with fear. It seems they were two graduates of Mount St Michael's, on vacation in Ireland, and they had set themselves up as judge and jury on the evidence of what they had read in the newspapers. As they were being hustled out by the management they screamed they would wait outside for me and would 'do me in' when I showed my face. Fortunately, there was another exit from the pub and I was able to make it safely to my car.

Mr McAntee, the Dublin barrister, arranged for me to acquire the help, and ultimately the counsel, of Michael Kennedy, a prominent New York City attorney. Mr McAntee had warned me that, if found guilty, I could face fifteen years in prison. He had been hired by the S.M.A. to represent my best interests, and his professional opinion was that my chances of getting justice in New York were minimal, especially in the homophobic climate fostered by the Reagan/Meese Administration. He advised me, in fact, to go to London and change my identity as the only way to protect myself.

However, I was determined to fight this to the end, and when Michael Kennedy agreed that my return was the wisest course, I went without delay. I had to clear my name – what was left of it – and try to undo the terrible wrong being done to my family and religious community. But most of all I wanted to protest the wrong being done to the gay and AIDS community, who were in many small, vicious ways being made to pay for the accusations levelled at me. It was my belief that the Archdiocese did not expect me to show for the trial, nor did they anticipate that my Order would pay the legal bills.

Of all the charges brought against the gay community there is none more common than the assumption that gay and paedophile are one and the same. People can hardly be blamed for this outlandish misconception when one considers how often the media, particularly the tabloid press, come out with it. *Some* gay people molest children, just as *some* heterosexual people do, but this is because they are emotionally and psycho-sexually damaged, whatever their sexual orientation. Such people desperately need psychological help (and sometimes the full force of the law) to protect their innocent victims. Although I now admit freely and willingly that I am gay I have never had any interest in forcing myself on anyone, sexually or otherwise.

My first impression of Michael Kennedy, my attorney, was his great professionalism. I met him at his office on Lexington Avenue and, once again, I had to go through the events of that evening when John Schaefer visited me. Mr Kennedy wanted to know everything: my precise relationship with John, how long I had known him, how had I gotten to know him, how much I knew about him, how often we had met, how often he had visited my apartment.

The outcome of this initial interview was that Mr Kennedy hoped he would have the whole case cleared up within six weeks. After all, it was a one-off, uncorroborated charge made by a highly disturbed young man, three years after the alleged event happened. Mr Kennedy couldn't have been more wrong. Thank God it was the last and only time he was to be wrong about anything concerning my case.

At this point I think it is important that I clarify my relationship with John Schaefer, who according to my attorneys was unduly influenced by the FBI in his accusation of my molesting him. The truth is that John Schaefer tried, in a sad, inept but wholly understandable way, to seduce me. I am aware that it sounds pretty fantastic that a fourteen-year-old boy should try to persuade a priest to have sex with him. But John, although only fourteen, was sexually very mature, and by his own admission gay. As Michael Kennedy pointed out in court, he had never received any love from his natural father, and in seeking that love from other adult males he was used and abused by them. He grew up believing that in order to receive affection he had to offer himself for sex. I had been aware of his need and of his disturbed state of mind. In fact, on the evening he visited me and suggested we have sex, he talked incessantly about wanting to go to Dignity so that he might meet other gay people. I pointed out that he was under age and that I would have to have written permission from his mother, or his guardian, to allow him to attend. And after he had made his desire for intimacy clear to me (his actual words were, 'I wouldn't mind having sex with someone as attractive as you'), and I had told him that such a relationship was both wrong and impossible, I also assured him that I was still his friend and was in no way deterred from my commitment to help him. And I was true to this promise. Later on I was to baptise his half-sister when his family could not find another priest because of the irregularity of his mother's marriage in the Church's eyes.

The day after the incident I called the head counsellor at the school and reported it to him. As far as I was concerned, the matter was closed. And, despite what he eventually did to me, I bear no malice towards the boy. I feel desperately sad for him. He, as much as I, was a victim.

Chapter
Ten

At first Mr Kennedy thought he would seek and obtain a dismissal of the charges. He wanted this not only for my sake but because he was genuinely worried about what a trial might do to young John Schaefer. This had been denied. It was, however, suggested that I could plea-bargain since many cases in the Bronx are settled this way, particularly those of this nature: a non-corroborated, first-time charge. It would have suited the prosecution perfectly, but I refused since to my mind to plea-bargain would be for me to admit guilt, and I was guilty of nothing. The Judge was understandably disappointed at my resistance. He called me and my attorney, together with the prosecution, to his private chambers.

Judge Roberts is a larger-than-life character. He is very theatrical, and cases that come before him invariably attract a lot of media attention. But he is a scrupulously honest and courageous man, as I was to find out. In his chambers that morning he told me to think of him as my Dutch uncle, out for my best interests. 'We all make mistakes. Now, Father, you can walk out of here a free man if you plead guilty to a misdemeanour. The Prosecution here, Mr Walsh, is willing, he informs me, to drop the criminal charges.'

It was very tempting. I was, quite literally, shaking. 'Your

Honour,' I said. 'I don't mean any disrespect but I cannot plead to anything because I am not guilty of anything.'

Judge Roberts jumped to his feet, and roared at the top of his voice, 'Then, Father, you risk going to jail, and by God, I'll send you to jail if you're found guilty of these charges.'

'But I didn't do anything, your Honour,' I pleaded.

'That's what they all say.'

'Your Honour, this is a set-up, a witch-hunt. A priest in the school died of AIDS. His brother, also a priest, started a public campaign to have me removed from the school. The organisation named SAFE [Students Against Faggots in Education] was founded to undermine my integrity –'

'Stop, stop, stop!' the Judge roared. 'What are you talking about – campaign? Witch-hunt? AIDS?'

I explained to him as best I could in the short time available. He looked genuinely taken aback, and turned to the Prosecution. 'Mr Walsh, did you know about this?'

'Yes, your Honour.'

'Oh. I see. Father Lynch, of course, you cannot plea.' He looked directly at me and said, 'I see.' Then he turned to Mr Kennedy. 'Is there anything else?'

'Yes, your Honour. Father Lynch would like his passport back so that he can return to Ireland for a holiday.'

'Granted.'

'Objection,' the Prosecution attorney said.

'Objection overruled,' said the Judge.

That over, it was decided that I would go for a non-jury trial. This gave Judge Roberts total control over my destiny.

Back in the courtroom both the decision concerning the type of trial I was to have, and the fact that my passport was to be returned were made public. My supporters formed a line by the court doorway to congratulate me. Judge Roberts, in his inimitably humorous way, requested wryly that the priest's 'receiving line' remove themselves to the hallway outside the courtroom.

It was to be ten months before the trial came to court. In that time there were several false starts, and several more attempts to derail the process. Each time there was the hope that the case, with such a flimsy basis, would be dismissed at the bench, and each time Mr Kennedy and the Prosecution argued the issues. I could not believe the case was not going anywhere, with the Archdiocese ignoring pleas from all sides. There were nuns writing to the Chancery about me: 'Why are you letting this man hang out there alone? He has served the church faithfully for almost twenty years.' There were also pleas to stop the trial registered by my superiors and by the Episcopal Bishop of New York, Dr Paul Moore. Robert Cammer, assistant to my attorney, suggested that I take a lie-detector test with one of the top experts in the country. I willingly did this and, according to the examiner, 'passed with flying colours'. Mr Cammer also presented the Clayton Motion to the Judge. This motion was a request on our behalf to have the charges dropped in the interests of justice to both the defendant and the Prosecution. But everything we tried failed to move the Prosecution from a head-on collision in court. John Schaefer, despite our urgent attempts to prevent his destruction, was to be pitted against me in what I was convinced was a stonewalling of our efforts to reveal what was hidden behind their behaviour, and no one, from the Cardinal Archbishop to the Prosecution, seemed to care what the human cost would be for either of us.

Finally, on April 18, 1989, the day of reckoning arrived. The event was a media extravaganza. They were all there: every major network in the city, and all the press. The courtroom was packed. The show, as they say, was on.

Chapter
Eleven

There is little doubt that had the accused been anyone but myself the case would have attracted practically no attention. It was just another tawdry, sordid little case, one of many such that were dealt with regularly by the courts. My case, however, drew manic publicity because of my character, profile and reputation. I was, in a word, famous – some would say infamous – for my work with people suffering from AIDS, but perhaps more for my well publicised stand in favour of gay rights in direct opposition to the Catholic Archbishop of New York. I had appeared on so many chat shows that I was, in a sense, a 'star'.

Bob Teague, the WNBC-TV reporter, accurately explained what the situation was all about. 'Every TV station in the town, radio stations, written press and so on – we all had formed opinions. We had all heard stories about those priests, you know, who are celibate – ha, ha, ha! I think there was a general belief, early on, that a dirty old man had been caught, and let's hope they hang him. This is understandable when you consider that in New York City, as a working journalist, you become pretty damn cynical. It costs the city so much damn money to bring someone to trial that they have to be very, very certain as a rule, and they have to spend all that money and the resources of the

city to try and put the accused away. We go into the court —
the media, that is — assuming that most offenders are guilty.
I mean — that is the reality.'

So, in the minds of many people I was guilty even before
the trial began.

Sean Walsh, the prosecuting attorney, made his opening
speech. I quote this, as I will most other statements at the
trial, directly from the official court transcript.

MR WALSH: Your Honor. This case involves one victim
named John Schaefer who was being counseled by
the defendant, Father Lynch, while he attended Mount
St Michael's Academy here in the Bronx. He was a friend
of Father Lynch. He was a friend of Father Lynch both
before and after this incident. He was someone who went
to Father Lynch because of his troubled background, his
family. He went to Father Lynch because of his own
question of sexual orientation.

This is a case where he placed his trust in a person who
was not only counseling him, but was a Catholic priest
in a Catholic institution. This does not involve issues of
sexual orientation either of Father Lynch, John Schaefer,
or anyone else because the time when this happened in
January 1985, John Schaefer was a minor.

THE COURT: How old was Mr Schaefer?

MR WALSH: He was, I believe, fourteen at the time . . .
John Schaefer will be called to testify and describe how
he went up to Father Lynch's apartment, after leaving
his girlfriend's house, to discuss some paper they were
writing. There was a relationship that had been going
on for quite some time where there was counseling,
friendship and trust placed in Father Lynch.

While he was in that apartment Father Lynch made
advances to him. He said he would leave the Order. 'We
could live together, we could sleep together.' He got on
top of John Schaefer, reached down into his clothing
and touched his genitalia. He took John Schaefer's hand

while he was on top of him on the floor and placed
John Schaefer's hand inside of his pants ... After a
short struggle John Schaefer got out from underneath
Father Lynch and told him he was not interested. John
Schaefer was in shock. It was not until several years later
that Agent McDonald of the FBI came and spoke to
John Schaefer while he was conducting an investigation
at Mount St Michael's, that, for the first time, John
Schaefer revealed what had happened.

I point out to the Court that in this – I mean, he
still remained friendly and unvindictive toward Father
Lynch, but in speaking to Agent McDonald, an experienced investigator in these matters, he revealed what he
had to say for the first time. I point out to the Court
that when Agent McDonald spoke to John Schaefer
he did not anticipate or know about this particular
incident, nor was he put on to this particular witness,
John Schaefer, by anyone at the school, either teachers
or anyone in authority there, but by a fellow student who
said it might be interesting to talk to John Schaefer.

I think this is important for the Court to note in
hearing this case and keep in mind during the course
of the testimony.

THE COURT: The purpose is merely to tell me what you
intend to prove. That may be something you can use
in argument and summation. All I am interested in is
what you intend to prove.

MR WALSH: We intend to prove that there was no
vendetta here. We intend to prove that there was no
attempt to get Father Lynch by anyone in the school,
or any attempt by the FBI to do so. In fact, this was
an interview of a young man who is now ready to
reveal what he said. To say and stand up and testify.
You'll hear testimony not only from Schaefer but also
from Agent McDonald with respect to this, and we
feel at the end of the case, after hearing from both
these witnesses, we would prove this case beyond a

reasonable doubt to the trier of the facts of this case, yourself.

Judge Burton Roberts then asked my attorney, Mr Kennedy, if he wanted to say anything.

MR KENNEDY: The evidence will show, Judge, that the complaining witness, this young man of fourteen or fifteen years at the time, now nineteen or twenty, is a very emotional, highly disturbed young man who was, in fact, victimized by a member of his own family, victimized sexually, your Honor, and it was that very sexual abuse by a member of Mr Schaefer's family that ultimately brought him to a position where he felt comfortable enough to be able to sit down with Father Lynch and to receive counseling from Father Lynch.

The evidence will show that Father Lynch has never been accused of impropriety of any sort in his eighteen years as an ordained priest. Most significantly with Mr Schaefer the evidence will show – as it frequently does in a case where an individual is troubled, is inadvertently dissembling or is admittedly lying or unable to tell what is the truth – that he tells a variety of stories. We'll point out to the Court that we have, essentially, three versions of this alleged event from Mr Schaefer. The first comes when he talks to Agent McDonald of the FBI, as my colleague, Mr Walsh says, several years after the event. His second version comes in his testimony to the Grand Jury, different in some critical particularities, your Honor, from the first statement.

The third version comes in a form of a verified civil complaint filed here in the Bronx Supreme Court in the early part of this year seeking five million dollars' damages from Father Lynch for the alleged victimization that the young man had experienced. That suit, the evidence will indicate, that suit was dismissed with prejudice after my colleague and I served a series of subpoenas on friends of Mr Schaefer whom our investigations had indicated might have relevant information with reference to it. So, we have three inconsistent statements.

The other thing that the defence will focus on for your Honor's consideration is the difference between what he (John Schaefer) says and the way he acts.

Mr Kennedy then went on to give the Court relevant details of my background: where I was born, where I was educated, when I was ordained, how I had served as a missionary in Africa, how I was requested to come to New York, how I involved myself administering to PWAs in New York. This, he said, was 'very similar to his missionary work, because as the evidence will show, in this day and age ministering to AIDS patients is not unlike ministering to lepers in years past.' He further pointed out that 'a smear campaign began at Mount St Michael's.' There was a good deal of rumour and innuendo and allegations about sexual impropriety involving victimised students and sexually promiscuous members of the faculty. He made it clear that 'those rumours, that campaign, eventually embroiled Father Lynch, not because Father Lynch was suspected by anyone of having abused anyone but because Father Lynch was a focus of an AIDS controversy in this archdiocese.'

Mr Kennedy also told the Court that I resigned from Mount St Michael's in December 1984:

This resignation, your Honor, was accepted at a time when there was no blemish on his career or record whatsoever. It was accepted notwithstanding the fact that ninety-eight percent of the faculty in St Michael's community supported Father Lynch and asked that he stay . . . but he resigned because the controversy was making it impossible for him to carry on his ministry to the young students. So he left.

THE COURT: Let me interrupt you there for a moment.

You indicated to me that he resigned as Campus Minister in Mount St Michael's in December of 1984?

MR KENNEDY: That is correct.

THE COURT: As I understand it the allegation contained in this indictment deals with the year 1985?

MR KENNEDY: January of 1985, that's correct, one month after Father Lynch's resignation.

THE COURT: I want to make sure the dates are correct.

MR KENNEDY: The dates are correct. The significance of them is going to require some filling in with evidence. We hope to be able to do that for you. What is significant about December 1984 is that it was the last month that Mr Schaefer was at Mount St Michael's because in January 1985, after a brief effort to get into Salesian High School, he found himself at the New Rochelle Academy, now defunct, a private academy high school. So that's where he was enrolled at the time of the alleged incident. So at the time of the alleged incident Father Lynch is no longer Campus Minister. John Schaefer is no longer a student at Mount St Michael's, but is in fact a student at New Rochelle.

The evidence will show that John Schaefer is a loner at the school. John Schaefer had not many friends but those friends were all adult men. In addition to having been abused by a member of his own family, John Shaefer became kind of prissy and indrawn. His relationships became concentrated on adult males and, indeed, at Mount St Michael's, he had adult male relationships as the evidence will show. So, when he would come to Father Lynch for counseling Father Lynch was one of the few people on whom he could rely, to whom he could tell of the terrible ordeal at home and, indeed, some of the ordeals he was experiencing at Mount St Michael's.

John Schaefer claims that he kept quiet about this alleged incident because he was afraid and didn't know what to do. He was afraid, and the reason he was afraid comes out in the Grand Jury testimony. He was afraid because he had been abused at home, and he was afraid of the reaction of his grandfather because it was, in fact, his grandfather's son, his own uncle, who had victimized him at a very young age, and that victimization had continued over many years, until he finally got out of the household. He's a victim of a broken home. His parents were divorced early on. He never saw his father. He lived with his grandmother, grandfather and uncle. He missed his mother. He had many things going against him, but the inconsistent story and the inconsistent conduct is what we ask you to focus on because it is that conduct that will show the incredibility of the story, and again I'm not suggesting deliberate lying but the incredibility of the young man's story will be patent, and these vicious charges which Father Lynch has had to live with for so long – we think we'll find to have been not proven and at the end of our presentation you will enter a verdict of not guilty. Thank you.

The prosecution began by calling Special Agent McDonald, and establishing his credentials. He was an attorney admitted to practice in the Commonwealth of Massachusetts. He graduated from Boston College Law School. He had a Master's degree in criminal law from New York University School of Law. He was currently completing his Master's in Art Education at Fordham University in the Bronx, and expected to get his Master's Degree in Sociology in the summer of 1989. Agent McDonald had worked with the New York City police in investigating sex crimes against children. He had received special training, and had lectured widely on the subject. He had qualified as an expert in the sexual exploitation of children. He was then asked to give the Court a 'brief scenario' as to what he did concerning the Mount St Michael's investigation.

AGENT MCDONALD: After meeting at the District Attorney's Office on June 30, 1987, we conducted a number of interviews with administrators, teachers and students at Mount St Michael's Academy in the Bronx, and during the course of this investigation we interviewed over thirty people, I would guess, in attempting to determine if any violations of criminal law on either the Federal or the State level had occurred.

Q: And did there come a time when you interviewed John Schaefer?

A: Yes, that's correct. I did.

Q: How did you come to interview John Schaefer?

A: During the course of our investigation, as we interviewed administrators and students at the school, we would ask for the names of anyone they thought we should interview during the course of our inquiry. I believe it was on July 14, 1987, I interviewed a student by the name of Robert Shaw, and Robert Shaw indicated that it would be beneficial to our investigation to interview John Schaefer.

Q: Other than Mr Shaw, had anyone else mentioned to you, whether teachers or administrators or anyone else, John Schaefer as someone you should speak to?

A: No. No one had.

THE COURT: And you saw thirty people, you interviewed these thirty people, and I assume that you asked these thirty people who they thought could give you some insight into that which you were investigating?

A: That's correct, your Honor.

THE COURT: And the only one of those thirty people that suggested that you interview John Schaefer was Robert Shaw, is that correct?

A: At that stage of the investigation, that's correct, your Honor.

THE COURT: Proceed.

Q: Now, when did you conduct an interview with John Schaefer?

A: Approximately ten days after interviewing Mr Shaw, I interviewed Mr Schaefer, and that would have been on July 24, 1987.

Q: Without telling us what he said to you, did he give you certain information?

A: Yes, that's correct. He did.

Q: And did he indicate if he had given that information regarding this alleged offence to anyone else prior to his conversation with you?

A: The indication was that he had never divulged this to anyone other than myself.

Q: And who else was present when you conducted this interview?

A: It was just myself and John Schaefer.

Q: In your experience, Special Agent McDonald, is it unusual for someone to relate such an incident to someone after such a long period of time?

A: Not at all.

MR KENNEDY: Objection.

THE COURT: Sustained. Strike out the answer.

For the rest of the time that the Prosecution had Agent McDonald on the stand, Mr Walsh quizzed him about his knowledge of my age and that of John Schaefer to clarify that I was an adult while John Schaefer, at that time, was a minor. Then Mr Kennedy set about questioning the Agent. Very quickly he established that it was more than just a casual interview that had brought Robert Shaw, and consequently John Schaefer, to the investigator's attention:

Q: On June 30 you were called to a meeting here with the Bronx District Attorney's Office, were you not?

A: Yes, that's correct.

Q: A couple of representatives from the Bronx District Attorney's Office were at the meeting, weren't they?

A: Yes, that's correct.
Q: They brought to your attention information that had been provided them by three present or former teachers at Mount St Michael's, is that correct?
A: Yes, that's accurate.
Q: Those gentlemen's names were Frank Hughes, Albert Poppeti, and Pagnozzi –
A: Joseph Pagnozzi, that's correct.

Agent McDonald was forced to admit that he opened a file on the matter purely on the 'information' provided by these three teachers. Not only that, although the agent did his best to hedge the issue it soon became evident that it was one of these teachers, Joseph Pagnozzi, who had suggested to him that he interview Robert Shaw.

Q: And ultimately you got the name of a young man named Robert Shaw, is that correct?
A: Yes, Mr Kennedy.
Q: And do you know from whom you got the name Robert Shaw?
A: I'm not entirely certain.
Q: If I suggested to you that it came from Mr Pagnozzi, would that sound correct to you?
A: It could well likely be.
Q: All right. And when you go to see Mr Shaw, Mr Shaw himself has no direct evidence or knowledge of any sexual impropriety, does he?
A: No, he does not.
Q: What he does suggest to you is that maybe if you go see Mr John Schaefer, Mr John Schaefer may have some evidence to give, or something to tell you that might further your investigation, correct?
A: Yes, that's correct.
Q: So when you go to see Mr Schaefer all you know about Mr Schaefer – and correct me if I'm wrong in characterizing the state of your knowledge – all you

know about Mr Schaefer is that Mr Shaw thought that
a conversation with Mr Schaefer might prove fruitful,
correct?

A: That is correct.

Under questioning it was further revealed that Agent McDonald
had been given two other names by Robert Shaw, the names
of two teachers, one of them a Brother Brady who, Agent
McDonald claimed, was the main focus of his investigation, not I.

Q: So, you went to John Schaefer's home and told him
you were interested in talking to him?

A: Yes I did.

Q: What did you tell him?

A: That the joint FBI and New York City Police Department sex exploitation of children Task Force was conducting an inquiry into criminal wrongdoings at Mount
St Michael's Academy.

Q: So you focused his attention on Mount St Michael's?

A: Absolutely.

Q: Did you focus his attention on any people at Mount
St Michael's?

A: Initially, no.

Q: Now, we've established that at the time you had
two names given you by Shaw, correct?

A: Yes.

Q: Did you focus young John Schaefer on either of
those two names?

A: Not initially, no.

Q: Neither of those two names was Father Lynch,
was it?

A: That's correct, it was not.

Q: Did you focus John Schaefer on what it was about
Mount St Michael's that you were interested in inquir-
ing about?

A: Yes I did.

Q: And tell us the words you used to so focus his attention.

A: That we were conducting an investigation into allegations of sexual misconduct at the school.

Q: Did Mr Schaefer say anything in response to your general focus statement?

A: Yes he did.

Q: What did he say?

A: Essentially that he had attended the school for an abbreviated period of time and initially, you know, he wasn't able to provide any information with particularity concerning Brother Brady, who was the main focus of the investigation.

Q: Then the conversation continued, did it?

A: Yes, that's correct.

Q: What was next said by you?

A: I asked him if there were any incidents or anything that happened in the school with respect to administrators or members of the faculty that he wanted to tell me about.

Q: Of any kind, or just –

A: General type, yes. I tried not to lead him.

Q: And what did he say in response to that?

A: He indicated that there were things that had happened that he never divulged to anyone before, and because he was upset and didn't know what to do about it, he was going to share them with me.

Q: And this was you and he alone?

A: Yes, we were alone, and in an FBI automobile in City Island.

Q: So when you met him in his house you didn't stay in his house, but you went out in the car?

A: That's correct.

Q: And no one was with you – you were alone.

A: The two of us, yes.

Q: Is that customary procedure?

A: Not uncustomary.

Q: But don't you routinely take a brother officer along with you on an inquiry or an interrogation such as this?

A: We don't interrogate people. This was not an adversarial contact so there was no reason to.

Q: You say the FBI never interrogates people?

A: Occasionally.

Q: Occasionally. Good. So, the two of you drove somewhere on City Island?

A: That's correct.

Q: And parked the car?

A: That's correct.

Q: Did you pick the spot?

A: Yes.

Q: Then you began your interview of him, yes?

A: Yes.

Q: Okay. Now at some point during the course of that interview the name Bernard Lynch came up for the first time, right?

A: That is correct.

Q: And it didn't come from you, did it?

A: No it did not.

Q: Because you had no information suggesting any criminal misconduct on Bernard Lynch's part, is that correct?

A: That would be accurate.

Q: So the sole source of the initial information about Bernard Lynch is John Schaefer, right?

A: About criminal misconduct, yes, sir.

Agent McDonald then was made to tell the Court what John Schaefer had told him. That is to say, John Schaefer's version of what had happened on the evening he visited my apartment, the version already outlined by the Prosecution. That said, Mr Kennedy continued his questioning.

Q: How long did this interview take? That is, how long

did you and John Schaefer stay in your car parked in this position on City Island?

A: I would estimate about an hour and a half.

Q: And at the termination of the interview, how did it end? How did you leave it? What did you say to Mr Schaefer about what the future might hold for you and him in terms of this interview?

A: I would have told him, or told him, that I was investigating this, and that the results would be presented to the Bronx District Attorney's Office or whatever tribunal would have jurisdiction.

Q: Now, you asked other people whether or not they could give you the names of people who might lead you to additional information – standard procedure in an investigation, correct?

A: Yes, sir.

Q: I assume you asked the same question of Mr Schaefer. Did you say something like, 'Well, John, you've told me this story about Father Lynch, now do you know anyone else who could give us anything on Father Lynch?' Did you ask him something like that?

A: You presume correctly, Mr Kennedy. Yes I did.

Q: All right. What did he say?

A: He indicated the name of another student that he thought we should interview.

Q: That's a young man by the name of Lofrumente, correct?

A: That's correct. Peter Lofrumente.

Q: You went to talk to Peter Lofrumente?

A: I did indeed, Mr Kennedy.

Q: He didn't have any stories of sexual abuse or criminal activity to ascribe to Father Lynch, did he?

A: No, he didn't.

Q: Did you ask Mr Schaefer when it was that he had last contacted or been contacted by Father Lynch?

A: I believe I did.

Q: And what did he respond to that?

A: It was my recollection that they continued to have an ongoing relationship or friendship.

THE COURT: Just so there's no misconception here, you described a conduct of sexual contact between Schaefer and Lynch: is that what Schaefer said?

A: Yes, your Honor.

THE COURT: And did you at any time ask him whether or not this sexual conduct, this act that he described to you, ever took place prior thereto or subsequent to the time he described?

A: Uh, with respect to the ongoing relationship?

THE COURT: Yes.

A: It was my impression that the conduct had taken place in the middle or, you know, during the ongoing relationship, your Honor.

THE COURT: Well, did you specifically ask the question?

A: I don't believe I specifically —

THE COURT: In other words you questioned Mr Schaefer. He described an act of sexual conduct with Father Lynch and you did not pursue or did not ask whether or not such sexual conduct ever occurred prior to the incident with Father Lynch or subsequent to the incident with Father Lynch?

A: No, your Honor, this was the only incident he related.

THE COURT: Proceed.

Q: Go back to that interview for just a minute. Mr Schaefer, at the time he described this alleged sexual activity with Father Lynch, he makes it clear to you, does he not, that he doesn't want this to happen, that he's upset by it, correct?

A: Yes, that's accurate, Mr Kennedy. He said he was upset.

Q: As a matter of fact Mr Schaefer said he got hysterical and started to cry?

A: I recall him saying he was crying.

Q: Did you ask Mr Schaefer how he got home that night from Father Lynch's apartment?
A: I don't recall expressly asking him that, no.
Q: If I suggested to you that he got a ride home that night from Father Lynch, that wouldn't surprise you, would it? As a matter of fact that conforms to the information you have, doesn't it?
A: I'm not aware of how he got home, Mr Kennedy.

It had gone well for us so far, and as I sat there I prayed that things would continue to go well. I dreaded the moment when John Schaefer would be put on the stand to testify since I knew he would never be able to stand up to the questioning. Aware of John's problems, I thought to myself how difficult it would be for him in this situation not to lie, and probably compound his already far too nervous state.

The Prosecution tried to delay calling Schaefer by saying it was already late in the afternoon. Judge Roberts agreed, but said as there was still twenty minutes or so he wanted him sworn in.

My reaction when John took the stand was one of great and genuine sorrow. I longed to be able to say to him, 'John, how could you lower yourself to this? What did I ever do to you to make you level such vile and untrue accusations against me?'

I remember how nervous he seemed, and how he never once looked in my direction. The Judge was kind and considerate to him. After he was sworn in the Judge said, 'All right, Mr Schaefer, just so you understand, there will be no filming and no audiotaping while you're on the stand.'

A: I understand.
COURT: You want to speak clearly, I want you to speak so that everyone can hear you, District Attorney, Defense counsel, defendant, myself.
A: Yes.
COURT: If there's a question you can't understand,

indicate that you don't understand and I'll have it rephrased for you.

A: Okay.

COURT: All right, you can step down, Mr Schaefer.

A: Thank you.

COURT: All right, we'll stand in recess now at the request of both sides to 11 a.m. tomorrow morning. Thank you very much. Good evening.

Chapter
Twelve

The veteran WNBC-TV reporter Bob Teague, who had admitted he had gone to the trial expecting to cover just another story 'about a dirty old man and a kid' later admitted that he found the whole thing 'mind-boggling'. And it certainly was. Bob Teague explained it best. 'It was, remember, a non-jury trial so you have the Judge in full control, and you had some of the most sensational theatrics that you've ever seen on the witness stand. It was almost like a Perry Mason movie, so to speak. I mean, here was this witness, the complainant, a Mr Schaefer, who would have convulsions and fits, and couldn't talk and couldn't stand and couldn't walk, blubbering and so on. Expert witnesses come in and say, "Well the man, the young man is so distraught he can't go back on the stand", and so on, but yet he has made these dramatic accusations. Now is this young man shamming as was suggested by the Judge on occasion, or is he for real? Then you have the efforts of the Prosecutor to give this young man time to recover to get back on the stand. Would he recover or wouldn't he? I've never seen anything like it before. Father Lynch was a target. He had worked with AIDS patients, gays etc. That's what it was all about, and this finally became apparent in the end.'

Sadly, it was to take three days before this did become

apparent, and in those three days I had to sit in silence and suffer as John Schaefer was made to suffer. It was evident from his attitude that John no longer wanted to testify; it was later to emerge that he had been groomed and cajoled into giving evidence. But he simply could not back out of his own volition. Once the District Attorney had filed charges the whole episode had to go to trial. As Judge Roberts was to admit, 'A Grand Jury may very well indict a ham sandwich at the behest of the District Attorney, though here, in Bronx County, we prefer to use a pastrami sandwich.' I, in this case, was the pastrami.

The second day of the trial opened with an off-the-record conference at the bench between the two attorneys and the Judge. It concerned a letter which John Schaefer had given to his attorney the previous afternoon, a copy of which Mr Walsh had now given to my attorney, Mr Kennedy. In this letter Schaefer clearly expressed his reluctance to testify, so much so that he intended to invoke the Fifth Amendment (the right not to testify). After a short consultation with me Mr Kennedy decided we should try once more to end the whole fiasco and save Schaefer from being exposed to the gruelling examination that would have to follow.

Mr Kennedy addressed the Judge: 'If I may, your Honour. Having read the statement it is clear to me that at least from the standpoint of Mr Schaefer he does not want to testify. He feels he is being forced to testify by the District Attorney, and by the FBI. He has indicated that he intends to take the Fifth Amendment. If he takes the Fifth Amendment after direct examination that would be totally inappropriate and obviously my direct would be dismissed. The problem with that is that it will be read into the record. The media will have heard it. I would again ask your Honour to answer my application to the Court to dismiss this charge.'

Unfortunately, the Prosecution would have none of that. Mr Walsh stated that he had spoken to John Schaefer that morning and that it was his intention now 'to go forward in this case and he wishes to testify. I will, in fact, explore this very issue with him at the beginning of my direct examination and he's not going to take the Fifth Amendment. He has committed no crime. He used that as an excuse so as not to testify. He doesn't wish to describe what happened to him. I think that can be understood as a natural concern.' And so John Schaefer was made to take the stand.

To begin with, the Prosecution's direct examination was straightforward enough, and John was cocky. He was, as he later confessed, 'performing' to the gallery of TV cameras although these were not being used to film him, on instruction from the Judge. John's background was gone into in some detail: his early childhood, how he had been abused, his days as a student at Mount St Michael's. He admitted that I had been the only one he felt he could trust, trust enough, that is, to speak of his confused sexuality. He admitted that I had spent several hours counselling him, admitted that I had 'been like a father' to him. However, as the questioning came closer to the time when he would have to answer concerning the alleged incident, he became more agitated, although maintaining a certain cheekiness.

Q: How many times did you go up to Father Lynch's apartment?
A: I was only there twice.
Q: You were only there twice. Could you describe his apartment?
A: Yes. You want me to describe the visual?
Q: Yeah, whatever.
A: Okay. You went in a long hallway, I remember like the first time I was there, something that took me back, was on the right-hand wall there was a large picture, it was entitled Hermaphrodite and it had sort of like heavy fisherman's net around it. From this picture you could tell that this boy, or girl, you couldn't tell that, had a breast exposed, and that there was a penis on this individual.

Q: And this is — you're saying now as you come in from the hallway?

A: That's right. It's on my right.

Q: Continue through the apartment.

A: It was just a long hallway, on your left was the bedroom, you went down and there was a living room, okay? In the living room there was a couch against the far wall, some shelving unit, and like on the edge of the shelving unit were other — I think the word you might use was explicit, nude men and women in these pictures. Not in sexual intercourse, but in — they were naked.

At this juncture the Prosecution abandoned this line of questioning, letting it hang so that the media and the Judge would be left with the impression that my apartment was filled with lewd pictures. And having set this scene he swiftly moved to asking about the alleged incident.

A: So I went up to his apartment, he answered the door, normal greeting, we hugged each other, and he asked how I was. He was — he was — I interrupted him during dinner, and he was drinking.

Q: Around what time was this?

A: I would say it was after dark, maybe like dusk, seven, seven p.m., eight o'clock. And there was wine on the table, and he asked me if I wanted any wine, and, you know, I said no, but I think he poured it anyway. And when I was — when I was there, we talked about a lot of stuff. He didn't clear the table, but he went to sit on the couch. So I went over to him, over to the couch and talked to him, and that's when the incident occurred. That's when he started, like, to touch my leg . . . And then he started to, like, roughhouse, like, you know, push back and forth, and he, like, pulled me down on the floor, and I was — we were on the floor, and I was on top of him, and I was being held there with his — like, his arms wrapped around me while he was using

90

his other hand to, like, grope at my pants, to grope at my pants – on the outside of the pants.

Then I – I was, like, getting really upset here, and I didn't know what to do, and I was asking him to stop, please stop, this is not something I wanted. First of all I was confused. I would never, ever, ever think of having sexual relationships with an older man who I regarded as somebody who would give me guidance, sort of like a father figure, and I was saying that, no, no, please stop, no, stop. And then he forced my hand down his pants, and I took it out and he forced it back down and I took it out and he forced it down again. He was trying to get me to masturbate him, and he did get my hand down his pants again, and I took it out, and he had his own hand down my pants, and this went on for a few minutes, and I finally got up to break away, and as I got up to the window with the radiator beneath it I realized my pants were opened and I was, like, heaving and crying. I was never so upset as at that moment in my life. The only time I can remember crying so hard was when my grandmother passed away.

And when I was there at the window, I was, like, no, I want to go home, I want to go home, and he was telling me that it wasn't wrong, that he would leave his order, that he wanted to have a relationship with me. He said he had done this before with a lot of friends, and he didn't mention any –

THE COURT: That's what he said?

A: Yes. And that it wasn't wrong, that he wanted to have a relationship with me, and he tried to convince me to stay over. Finally after about five minutes of him still being on the floor, he got up, took a few minutes, I believe he cleared the stuff off the table, and he said you want to take a cab home, or whatever, but he had agreed earlier to drive me back home to my grandparents, and after a long time, like a long time being twenty minutes when you're in that situation, a long time is a minute, and he finally drove me home and it was a pretty — pretty quiet car ride home.

I was shattered. I listened to John recount a total fairytale. It was clear that the Court was believing him. It had gone very quiet. I could hear my own heart thumping. I remember putting my hand on it, trying to deaden the noise.

After establishing that John told no one about this incident, no one in his family, that is, the Prosecution turned its attention to his meeting with Agent McDonald.

Q: John, you said you went home and didn't tell anyone about the incident. When was the first time you mentioned this incident with Father Lynch to anyone?
A: To Al McDonald in the summer of 1987, on City Island.
Q: So between the day of the incident and meeting Al McDonald you had told no one about what happened?
A: No. I had asked questions to a friend of mine, Peter Lofrumente, as if, like, you know, in a general sense, like, if anything had ever happened like this, or if he had ever heard anything.
Q: So, you did relate to Agent McDonald what happened to you?
A: Yes. We spoke I believe for an hour and fifteen minutes, and in that period of time he asked me to go through a school yearbook and see if I could recognize anybody, and I told him — I told him that a sexual misconduct had been conducted with myself, and I had not said anything about it to anyone, and the incident happened in 1985, and this was early 1987, and I had not said anything to anybody, but I — I can't tell you why I did it, but I did it, and it was the truth, it was not something I made up on the spur of the moment. Father Lynch was a part of my life up until then.

Q: Did he specifically ask you about Father Lynch or –

A: No.

Q: In other words –

A: It was a generality. He asked if I knew about any sexual misconduct amongst the faculty without mentioning any names, asked me to go through the yearbook, do I recognize anyone, did I hear any stories, so he could go on and conduct his investigation.

THE COURT: And he gave you no specific names?

A: No.

THE COURT: And then you stated the incident which occurred at the end of January –

A: Yes.

THE COURT: Of 1985, or the beginning of February, either one, right?

A: Yes.

Q: Did you tell him when you had this first initial interview, did you follow up and have other interviews with him, and discussions?

A: Not really. After the initial interview I had a couple of meetings with Mitch Garber who was the original Assistant D.A., but there would be, like, month intervals, it was very slow-moving over the past two years, and as far as meeting with Al McDonald, Special Agent McDonald was, I believe, transferred to Boston, and that is why he wasn't so actively involved in the case. Most of my interaction was by telephone. It was with Detective Gelfand.

Q: During the time that you discussed with either McDonald for the short time he was still here, then later Detective Gelfand, and Mitch Garber, did you relate more information, background information, more details?

A: Yes.

Q: With the incident itself?

A: I'll state again that by talking about this, talking about it to friends and talking about it to my family – and not my whole family knew right away, I told my grandfather first, and then my grandmother found out only a few months ago, and I realized that there was more and more that I was remembering about what happened. It's something you put out of your mind, you don't think about it. So, like I said today, I could tell you more details as I talk through it than I told at the original interview.

Q: Is it fair to say that you were trying to block this incident from your mind and put it behind you?

A: Yes.

The Prosecution now brought up the letter that John Schaefer had given him the previous afternoon. It was handed to John, and he was told to read it. It had been entered as exhibit 70.

Q: I would ask you to particularly note in that exhibit any reference you make in there with respect to when you made this information first known to Agent McDonald.

A: Okay.

Q: Just look at it please, and then I'll ask the question.

THE COURT: You're asking him to look at the –

MR WALSH: I'm asking him to look at 70 with respect to a particular item.

THE COURT: With respect to see what that particular exhibit, which is not in evidence, says about that?

MR WALSH: That's correct, it's not in evidence. I'm asking him to look at it.

THE COURT: He's looking at it. Okay, what's the question?

Q: Did you ever subsequently state at any time that Agent McDonald referred to Bernard Lynch and it was he who first raised Father Bernard Lynch's name to you?

A: Yes. I allege that in this letter, but I want to state that I wrote this letter very quick –

THE COURT: Strike that. Don't answer any questions about that. You said you stated that in the letter?

A: Yes. I stated that in the letter.

Q: This was it?

A: I wrote this letter in anger. A lot of thoughts expressed in the letter is written. This letter was written in less than a minute and a half. I wrote this off and was just letting my thoughts flow. I even contemplated not giving it to you and I realized that what's written here I meant to be more general than the specifics and it is in error.

Q: John, after this incident occurred with Father Lynch, did you have any further contact with Father Lynch either in person or over the telephone?

A: Yes, over the phone. He was traveling a lot, I remember that, but when I went to ask him about it on the telephone he was just asking me about my life and what I was involved in. He did know I was in a relationship with somebody in Long Island. Also, in April 1986 I had called Father Lynch and told him that my grandmother had passed away and would he like to say a Mass at our church. He said he was unable to do that because he had a commitment for that day, but he would come to the funeral home and say a prayer over my grandmother's body. That was in April of 1986. The following year, I believe, it was April 1987, Father Lynch, because of my family, they respected him and – and he was a friend of mine, that they decided that they would want him at my sister's christening, if he was agreeable and my sister was christened. She was born October of 1986, so I believe it was, and he said the Mass for my sister's christening at our church in City Island.

THE COURT: You asked him?

A: Yes, I did.

Q: Would you tell Justice Roberts why you asked somebody who just attacked you sexually to do these things and why you maintained a relationship with him thereafter?

A: My relationship with Father Lynch was a longstanding one. Before the incident happened. The incident did happen and I denied it happened. I thought that, maybe, by some chance, I had done something wrong and felt guilty, but in relation to this, in retrospect, I'm looking back and saying, no, in my mind these incidents are getting larger and more frequent and the hugging and the touching and the sexual innuendos that was leading up to this, and I think he wanted me to make overtures to that, and that second time at the apartment, he wanted to go past that incident into some form of sexual relationship. I'm only taking that from an opinion and what could, like, could project to the future from what he had said to me there. He said he wanted a relationship. If it worked out he would be willing to leave his — the priesthood, so I feel that, now, that incident happened, I'm angry but, at the time before I brought up the incident again, I denied it before that June of 1987 — that early, that summer of 1987 interview with the FBI I was — I was denying it happened. I still wanted him to be a vital part of my life like it was a whole bunch of experiences and that this part was just one, but it didn't fit. I just wanted to deny that it was even there.

Judge Roberts interrupted at this point to establish in his own mind how many times John Schaefer had telephoned me, and how often we had talked. He also clarified that John and I had met on two occasions: once at the funeral parlour and again at the christening of his sister. He established that 'the incident' was never spoken about even though we had spoken some ten times on the telephone. John Schaefer admitted that on each of those ten occasions I wanted him to get some kind of counselling because 'he felt I needed it'. Then Mr Walsh continued his examination.

Q: Going back to the incident in April, John, you indicated that there was some wine there. Did you drink any wine when you were there?

A. I believe he poured it for me and I may have had a sip, but I did not finish it or drink the whole thing.

Q: Were you intoxicated on any drugs at the time?

A: No.

Q: Did you see Father Lynch drink any wine?

A: Yes.

Q: Did he appear to you sober? Was he intoxicated?

A: In my opinion, no, he wasn't.

THE COURT: Is that wasn't sober or wasn't intoxicated?

A: Wasn't sober.

THE COURT: Was his speech slurred?

A: Yes. He was, like, really shaky, like away. I had never seen him before –

THE COURT: What indication did you have, what evidence did you have that he was not sober? What did you observe?

A: I saw him drink two glasses of wine in my presence, but there was a carafe on the table that was, in a manner, half empty.

THE COURT: What did you see which caused you to come to this conclusion other than the incident that you spoke about?

A: I have to tell you that I know Father Lynch and I met with him for many days and I had never seen him like that before. He was in a different state of mind or a different – he was in a different manner, a different personality than I had usually observed him in.

THE COURT: Do you still want to proceed at this point?

MR WALSH: I don't have much more. I would like to finish before lunch.

THE COURT: All right.

Q: Do you feel, John, looking back on this date, did you try to seduce Father Lynch into this sexual relationship?

A: No.

Q: Did you bring a lawsuit – civil lawsuit against Father Lynch?

A: Yes I did.

Q: When was that?

A: In the last two months. I brought it before my birthday of this year because if I had waited after my birthday I couldn't have proceeded with the lawsuit.

Q: That was what your lawyer told you, correct?

A: Correct.

Q: Your lawyer, a private attorney in that case?

A: Correct.

THE COURT: Did you hire the attorney?

A: Yes – he's my girlfriend's father. I don't know if that matters.

Q: He was not procured for you by the District Attorney's Office or the Task Force, is that correct?

A: No, this was my own doing.

Q: Did there come a time when you decided not to go forward with the lawsuit?

A: It was not tossed out of court. I made a decision because of the further harassment that other people were being subpoenaed that I really didn't want to know what was going on. I didn't know it was getting so big and everything, and it passed into a lot of people's knowledge which, unfortunately, now, it's all over the news now, but I decided that I did not want it to be all over the news and that even though the possibility of a monetary compensation was not worth going through the harassment of reporters and Father Lynch's attorneys.

Q: Did you instruct your lawyer to discontinue the lawsuit?

A: That's correct.

Mr Walsh concluded by asking John Schaefer what his feelings were towards me now.

A: In retrospect, my relationship with Father Lynch as part of growing up, was very important to me. How that affects me at the moment is that, sure, I remember the good times, but even though I denied that bad thing happening, it did happen and now the truth is known. Whoever believes it or not, I know it happened, and I know that Father Lynch is going to deny it, and say that it's a whole bunch of people out to get him. It's not that. He did something wrong and should tend to that, and I feel that because he has lied and said that a lot of things I said that night that I never even said, I feel that, in my opinion of him up until the case was that I remember the good things. Those were the most important in my mind even though this case was coming up. But last night, especially when I heard on the news the things he said about me lying, and what he said I *did* say are not true, and I look at him as a liar now.

MR WALSH: I have no further questions.

The Judge warned John Schaefer not to talk to anyone outside his immediate family about the case. He then called a recess until 2.30 p.m.

Chapter
Thirteen

As I sat at the table beside Mr Kennedy waiting for the Judge to emerge from his chambers, I was filled yet again with that curious feeling that this was not happening to me. I was innocent, so it *could* not be happening to me. I remember glancing at Mr Kennedy. He was normally a cheerful man but now his face was grim, and he toyed with John Schaefer's letter. I had an overwhelming urge to beg him to take it easy; the boy had been used and manipulated by these so-called guardians of the law, and I felt desperately sorry for him.

Finally, Judge Roberts came from his chambers and the Court was again in session. John Schaefer was recalled to the stand, and it was clear that he was in a defiant mood. He looked cocky, almost as if he was enjoying himself. I wondered then, and I still wonder, if he fully realized the seriousness of the situation. It struck me that he was treating the trial as a show, a theatrical performance with himself in the starring role.

My attorney, Michael Kennedy, rose and strolled toward the witness stand. He was very casual, very polite, and spoke in a quiet, disarming voice. He asked John Schaefer if he would kindly remember the Judge's request earlier that day: that he speak up so that everyone could hear his answers, and that if he didn't understand a question he should indicate so immediately, when the question would be rephrased. Then he asked that a court officer hand John exhibit 70, the letter.

Q: You recognize that, do you not?

A: Yes I do.

Q: It's a handwritten statement prepared by you, Mr Schaefer, in the last couple of days, correct?

A: Yes it is.

Q: The same statement was presented to Assistant District Attorney Walsh yesterday?

A: Yes it was.

Q: And at the time you presented it to him, you meant everything that was in that statement, didn't you?

A: Yes.

Q: And at the time you *wrote* it you meant everything in that statement, didn't you?

A: No, I did not.

Q: You did not? So this statement contains some things you did mean and some things that you did not mean, is that correct?

A: That's correct.

Q: All right. Now, you testified to being harassed by the defense attorneys for Father Bernard Lynch?

A: Yes.

Q: Including myself?

A: Or agents there, of your office.

Q: You didn't mention in your testimony that you had been harassed by the Bronx District Attorney's Office?

A: No I did not.

Q: But that's in your statement, isn't it?

A: Yes it is.

Q: Is that true then — that you were harassed by the Bronx District Attorney's Office?

A: Harassed is a very harsh word, sir.

Q: Well, whose word was harassed, yours?

A: Yes.

Q: Anybody make you write that statement?

A: No.

Q: Anybody with you when you wrote it?

A: No. I wrote this of my own volition.

Q: Nobody coached you in the language?

A: No.

Q: So the language is entirely of your choosing?

A: Yes.

Q: Now, nowhere in your statement does it say that you felt harassed by Father Lynch, does it?

A: No.

Q: It *does* say that you felt harassed – by the Bronx D.A.'s Office, does it not?

A: Yes it does.

Q: It says, 'Each time I've mentioned that I don't want to be involved any more –'

Judge Roberts intervened at this point to establish clearly that John Schaefer had indeed written the letter. Mr Walsh objected to the letter being introduced, but was overruled. Mr Kennedy continued:

Q: I'm going to read from this letter and I want you to correct me if I make any mistakes.

A: Okay.

Q: Your words, Mr Schaefer: 'I'll begin by stating that I personally had no intention of going to the authorities and opening a case against Bernard Lynch. Although an unfortunate incident did take place several years ago, my intention was not to relive it in my mind, but to put it behind me and get on with my life.' That's the first part and that's correct, isn't it?

A: Yes it is.

Q: All right.

THE COURT: Correct insofar as he wrote it or correct about what it says?

Q: It's correct insofar as what you wrote and correct insofar as what you meant, isn't it?

A: No, it's not.

Q: No? Okay. Next paragraph –

The Prosecution again objected, trying to prevent his witness being crossexamined on it. 'If counsel wishes to read this aloud, he may do so, but my objection is this: he is proceeding to go through in asking this, it's already been authenticated with respect to what's in there.'

Judge Roberts said, 'Well, hear me for a moment. What he's trying to do, as I understand it, is to indicate and find out whether or not he [Schaefer] meant what he said. Now, possibly he can phrase the question so there's no ambiguity. You can ask him, if you wish, do you still feel as you did when you wrote it, or some other phraseology. I don't want to tell you how to phrase it.'

MR WALSH: Under those circumstances I withdraw my objection.

THE COURT: Okay.

Q: With reference to exhibit 70, you wrote it a couple of days ago, and you wrote what you intended to write, correct?

A: Correct.

Q: You wrote what you were feeling?

A: Correct.

Q: And you meant what you were writing?

A: At the time, correct.

Q: Right. What then happened was that you presented this document to some representative of the Bronx District Attorney's Office, correct?

A: Yes.

Q: Would that be Mr Sean Walsh?

A: Yes it would. Yes it would.

Q: And at the time you presented it to Sean Walsh, you meant the language that was contained in here, did you not?

A: Yes.

Q: Okay. But now after having presented it to Sean Walsh you no longer mean some of the things that are in here, correct?

A: That is correct.

Q: And this change in your own meaning comes as a result of conversations with Mr Walsh, does it not?

A: No, it does not.

Q: Does it come as a result of conversations with Mr Gelfand?

A: No it does not.

Q: Does it come as a result of conversations with anyone?

A: Yes it does.

Q: With whom?

A: With FBI Agent Jim Clementi, as well as my family.

Q: So. FBI Agent Clementi. He was able to persuade you that you did not mean what you wrote of your own volition?

A: No. No. No. Absolutely, absolutely not.

Q: Oh? Well, what changed your meaning, what caused you to change what you wrote and believed at the time you wrote it, and at the time you presented it to the District Attorney but you don't mean now, – what happened?

A: Those conversations were not a factor in my changing my mind. It was inside of me. It was a personal decision. I stated that before.

Q: Right. I understand. And what was it that happened inside of you, Mr Schaefer, can you explain that to us? What happened inside of you to cause you to mean one thing on one occasion but mean something else with the same language on another occasion?

With my parents in Ireland, 1947.

Aged eight with my brother Sean and my sister Mary.

With my parents, Sean and my sister Ruth, on the day I left home to study for the priesthood, September 15, 1965.

At my ordination, December 20, 1971.

On a communications course in Booterstown, Dublin, 1972.

Celebrating mass at the Kabushi Church, Ndola, Zambia, 1973/74.

After mass with my congregation in Zambia.

With my parents and friends after receiving my doctorate, 1980.

Marching in the New York City Gay Pride Parade, 1984.

Hearing confession at Mount St Michael's Academy,
New York.

With students at Mount St Michael's Academy.

Priest surrenders on sex rap

ATRICE O'SHAUGHNESSY

Daily News

Warrant issued for priest

Irish Voice

...rdale s...

Sex rap for priest at boys' school

The campus chaplain and the former acting principal ...ic high

New York Post

Irish Priest On Sex Charges

AN IRISH priest, Father Bernard Lynch from Ennis,

Irish Voice

Vatican Reproaches Homosexuals With a Pointed Allusion to AIDS

New York Times

Irish Echo

Irish priest on sex charge surrenders in New York

Pro-Gay Priest Accused of Sex Abuse

Activists Charge "Homophobic Witch-hunt"

New York Native

Irish Priest Surrenders To Bronx D.A.

By MAIRE CROWE

FR. BERNARD Lynch, the ...b-born M... ...priest...

Irish Voice

Witness Reports Fondling by Priest

By Ellis Henican   Roberts in the Bron... ...onvicted   about sex. "He was a touchy-feelie per-   chology paper. When he entered the
                                                                                                                        ...id, he couldn't help no-

Daily News

Irish Voice

Priest Claims He Was Framed

Irish Independent

Shaky prosecution shock

involved in sexual charges

Lynch Attorney Seeks Case Dismissal

Irish Voice

The Bronx

Priest found innocent of sexual abuse

on May 13 on charges he fondled   Walsh

Cork Examiner

The U.S.
Vindicated

ALL charges against Fr. Bernard Lynch, the

Daily News

AIDS fight priest is home

passed. I am not vindictive

Charges dropped against priest

ALL CHARGES against Father ever Judge Burton Roberts replied
B... that he was dismissing the

Irish Times

Irish priest acquitted on sex abuse charges

Hanlon

Irish Echo

Priest cleared in sex abuse

was mistaken and then from Long Island had been

Daily News

AIDS priest tells of injustice

By Damien McHugh

Innocent from the outset

The Sunday Tribune

Evening Press

During the filming of 'AIDS: A Priest's Testament', in Central Park, 1987.

With Bishop Paul Moore and Timothy Coughlin, President of Dignity, on the formation of an informal religious coalition to support the Gay Rights Bill before the City Council, 1987.

A: That document was written out of anger, okay, anger and confusion. I was very confused by my feelings as to whether or not I wanted to testify here. Getting it down on paper I realized that my anger — I was able to get it down on paper. Then I spoke to Jim Clementi. He did not tell me to testify. He did not tell me that the document was garbage. He told me about his feelings about other people involved in cases such as this.

Q: What did he tell you his feelings were, this FBI Agent?

MR WALSH: Objection. Can we have the witness finish his testimony before another question is asked?

THE COURT: Yes.

MR WALSH: Thank you.

MR KENNEDY: Please excuse me for interrupting.

A: And as far as the conversation with my family, I talked to them about the letter as well, and I said to them that I wrote down an angry letter, and that I wanted to get my feelings out on paper so I could get my thoughts together. This document, I wasn't even going to present this document to the Assistant District Attorney's office. I made the decision to testify before I even met with Sean Walsh yesterday, before the document was even in the building.

Q: What was it that Clementi, FBI Agent Jim Clementi, said to you that ultimately caused you to reconsider the language of Defense exhibit 70?

A: Your Honor, may I point out that my family's conversation came first, and then I was reconsidering, and when I spoke to Jim Clementi, and when he told me that other people were involved in cases like this and walked away from them, do not get the satisfaction that they told the truth, that is exactly what he told me.

Q: All right. So, FBI Agent Jim Clementi said you would not be satisfied if you did not go ahead and testify, correct?

A: My answer to that is no, FBI Clementi told me that . . .

Q: Take your time, Mr Schaefer.

A: Yes, I understand. Jim Clementi was telling me about other cases in which individuals who don't tell the truth and choose not to testify don't feel the satisfaction, or don't feel the sense of relief from testimony.

Q: And was FBI Agent Clementi successful in persuading you that you no longer meant all of this?

A: Not solo.

Q: Not by himself. Did FBI Agent Clementi contribute to the mental process going on within you that caused you from saying that you meant this on one occasion, and now are saying that you don't mean it?

A: Yes.

Q: Okay. Thank you. Now, I would like to go through the statement with you, and we'll go through it paragraph by paragraph, Mr Schaefer.

A: That's fine.

Q: I'd like you to read the first paragraph and then I've got a couple of questions about it. Read it in a good loud voice, please.

A: 'I will begin by stating that I personally had no intention of going to the authorities and opening a case against Bernard Lynch. Although an unfortunate incident did take place several years ago, my intention was not to relive it in my mind, but to put it behind me and get on with my life.'

Q: All right. Stop right there for a moment, please, Mr Schaefer. Now, the time you wrote that, you meant it, you intended it, and you felt it, correct?

A: Correct.

Q: Do you still feel it, mean it, and or intend it?

A: No.

Q: You don't?

A: No.

Q: Next paragraph. Read it, please.

A: 'A couple of years ago I was approached by Al McDonald of the FBI. I was told that there was evidence that Bernard Lynch had been sexually involved with some young boys, and they were getting a case together to present to the Grand Jury. They had gotten my name from the school's class roster during the time Bernard Lynch was there and asked me if I knew anything or had been involved. I answered truthfully, just as I subsequently answered those questions truthfully in front of the Grand Jury.'

Q: Now, Agent McDonald testified that he, Agent McDonald, never claimed that he was building a case against Bernard Lynch or that he suggested to you that he was building a case against Father Lynch. That was his testimony under oath yesterday.

A: Okay.

Q: All right.

THE COURT: That was your testimony as well, is that correct, when he saw you, he did not bring up the name of the Reverend Bernard Lynch?

A: That's correct. And I said that I made an error in this and my previous testimony, yes.

THE COURT: You were the one who initiated that conversation?

A: Yes. Yes, absolutely.

THE COURT: Were you ever told by Agent McDonald that there was evidence that Bernard Lynch had been sexually involved with some young boys and that they were getting a case together to present to the Grand Jury?

A: No, your Honor.

Q: But at the time you wrote this you meant it?

A: No . . .

Q: Excuse me . . .

A: Can I explain this, your Honor?

THE COURT: Yes you may.

A: I wrote this in less than a minute and a half. I was just writing my thoughts as they came to me. This did

107

happen, they were building a case against Bernard Lynch after the facts. I was just getting my facts confused and I was writing down what was coming into my mind like this.

THE COURT: Was it a mistake?

A: Yes, your Honor.

THE COURT: When you wrote that?

A: Yes.

THE COURT: This is not so, correct?

A: This is not correct.

THE COURT: All right.

A: Where it says that he had information, that they had gotten names from the school – sorry. Okay, where I was told there was evidence that Bernard Lynch had been sexually involved with some young boys and they were getting a case together for the Grand Jury was a mistake, your Honor.

THE COURT: It was not so?

A: No, it wasn't.

Q: And the reason you made that mistake was because you were angry, as I understand it?

A: That's correct.

Q: So, when you're angry you are capable of accusing someone such as FBI Agent McDonald of doing something that he didn't do at all, is that correct?

A: No. I also used the word confused. Angry and confused.

Q: So, when you're both angry and confused you can accuse someone such as an FBI agent of doing something that they didn't do at all? Can you answer my question, please, Mr Schaefer?

A: Yes. Yes.

Q: Go on, please, to the next paragraph, if you will. It begins with the language, 'I was told . . .'

A: I'm aware of that. I wrote it.

Q: Thank you. Good loud voice, please.

A: 'I was told that if I would help them with the case,

their case, not my personal case, that I would get a lot of support as other boys were being contacted and would undoubtedly come forward as I have.'

Q: Stop right there. Who told you that?

A: This was told to me by Mitch Garber when I first saw him.

Q: Mitch Garber?

A: Yes.

Q: Mitch Garber, for the record, was at that time an Assistant District Attorney in the Bronx District Attorney's Office, was he not?

A: Yes, he was.

Q: Now, is *that* the truth? That is, is that what the A.D.A. Mitch Garber told you, or is that something that you made up out of anger and confusion too?

A: No, it's the truth. Other boys were contacted.

THE COURT: No, no . . .

A: Yes, this statement is true. Yes.

THE COURT: Did A.D.A. Mitch Garber state that to you?

A: It was stated to me, but not only by Mitch Garber. It was stated to me by people involved in the case. Yes.

Q: Who else said this to you?

A: FBI —

Q: Agent McDonald?

A: Yes.

Q: Detective Joe Gelfand?

A: Yes.

Q: And A.D.A. Mitch Garber?

A: Yes.

Q: All these told you that if you would help them with the case . . . and then you say that's their case, not your personal case?

A: Right.

Q: 'That I would get a lot of support as other boys were being contacted and would undoubtedly come forward as I have' — right?

A: Yes.

Q: They did tell you that – so that's the truth?

A: Yes.

Q: So you did not write that portion out of anger and confusion, but you wrote that portion as an accurate recollection of facts?

A: Yes.

Q: So, there are times in the statement when you are writing out of anger and confusion, and other times when you are not, correct?

A: Yes.

Q: Sometimes in the statement you are in control, other times you were not, correct?

A: No.

THE COURT: Would it be fair to say that when you wrote the entire statement you were confused and angry, that some of that which you wrote is completely accurate, some of it not so accurate?

A: Could have slipped by me, yes. Yes.

THE COURT: Proceed.

Q: All right. Then there's an asterisk, and if you would read along the side of the paper, please, Mr Schaefer.

A: 'I was also told that cases like this one usually do not go any further than the Grand Jury, that the defendant would probably enter a plea once the Grand Jury presented their evidence.'

Q: Right. Did someone actually tell you that?

A: Yes.

Q: Who told you that?

A: People I mentioned before.

Q: Mitch Garber, Detective McDonald, Detective Joe Gelfand?

A: Yes.

Q: So therefore is it correct that at the time you originally told them this story about Father Lynch your expectation was that you could tell them this story in private and never have to come to court and tell this story?

A: That's correct.

Q: Now, getting back to the statement after the asterisk, back to the main text, would you read that next paragraph for us?

A: 'I was told in front of witnesses that if at any time I felt like I couldn't go through with it, I would be able to withdraw. Many times I approached the D.A.'s Office to stop the case, but they cajoled me into continuing' –

Q: Stop right there. Now, did somebody – did you actually approach them many times to stop this case?

A: Yes.

Q: And who was it you approached, Mr Schaefer?

A: A.D.A. Mitch Garber.

Q: Anyone else?

A: No.

Q: Okay.

THE COURT: Did they ever state to you that if you did not wish to go through with the case you could withdraw?

A: Yes, they did.

THE COURT: And was that the same party that told you, A.D.A. Mitch Garber?

A: Yes, it was.

Q: You go on to say that 'They cajoled me into continuing'.

A: Yes.

Q: Cajole is your word?

A: Yes.

Q: What does cajole mean?

A: I think of cajoled meaning they talked to me, and talked to me, and told me if I would go and agree to let them go forward with the plea, that the Father would accept the plea and the case would then end.

THE COURT: Would you say persuade?

A: Yes.

THE COURT: You find cajole and persuade synonymous?

A: Not quite synonymous, but close.

Q: Go on reading.

A: '— they cajoled me into continuing until Father Lynch took a plea. This was also said in front of witnesses. I emphatically stated at each of these discussions that I didn't want to testify, but would agree to let the D.A.'s Office seek a plea but I would not participate in a trial.'

Q: And that's accurate, is it not? That is what you told A.D.A. Garber?

A: Yes.

Q: Agent McDonald and Detective Gelfand?

A: Yes.

Q: 'I'll go through with this as long as I don't have to go to trial?'

A: Yes.

Q: As long as you didn't have to go public?

A: Yes.

Q: And what did they say to that?

A: They said, 'Let us go forth with the case and see what happens with the plea, and then the same statement from before still stands' — that if at any time I wanted to withdraw I could.

Q: Okay. Then go back to 'Months went by' — see that?

A: Yup.

Q: Read it, please.

A: 'Months went by without hearing a word. Then the FBI and New York City Police Department Detective Gelfand would call me and I would come in for a meeting with the D.A.'s Office. Months would go by again and I would suddenly hear from them again and another meeting would take place, including one at which I had to testify for the Grand Jury. Each time this happened I became more and more emotionally upset at having to relive the incident over and over again in front of other people. I've had to see a therapist over the situation.'

Q: All right. Now, that paragraph – that's all accurate, isn't it?
A: Yes.
Q: And you meant it?
A: Yes.
Q: That was not a product of confusion and anger?
A: This whole letter was – is a product of confusion and anger.
Q: I'm talking about this paragraph.
A: This whole letter.
THE COURT: This whole letter – you indicated in your testimony – is a product of confusion and anger. That last paragraph you just read was true when you wrote it?
A: Yes.
THE COURT: True when you gave it, and it's true today as you sit on the stand, is that correct?
A: Yes.
Q: Thank you, Mr Schaefer. Now, go to the paragraph beginning 'Recently', please.
A: 'Recently I have decided that I just cannot take any more of this emotionally. I also had a bout of spinal meningitis a short time ago, and both emotionally and physically I'm not up to this.'
Q: And that was accurate at the time you wrote it?
A: Yes.
Q: Accurate now?
A: Yes.
Q: And let me ask you, do you feel that you are now physically able to continue?
A: Yes, I do.
Q: Okay. Go on, please, the next paragraph.
A: 'Each time I've mentioned that I don't want to be involved any more, as I was promised I could do, I've been harassed by the Bronx D.A.'s Office, called names, told that I opened a big can of worms and now I looked like a big liar etcetera.'
Q: Stop there for a moment. Now, I assume that this

113

paragraph – that you've been harassed by the Bronx
District Attorney's Office, called names, and told that
you had opened a big can of worms is something that
you wrote out of confusion and anger?

A: That's correct.

Q: You certainly didn't mean that?

A: No. Yes. That happened. This isn't – this happened.

Q: This *is* true?

A: Yes, this happened.

Q: Oh, this *is* true, the Bronx D.A.'s Office harassed you?
You have to answer.

A: Yes.

For the first time the gasp from the courtroom was clearly
audible. I really don't believe that John Schaefer knew the
seriousness of what he was saying: the D.A.'s Office and the
FBI were publicly being accused, by their own witness, of
cajoling a reluctant witness to testify. Judge Roberts seemed
astonished. I suspect it was the first time he had ever heard
anything quite as blatant as this in all his days in court.
He was determined to make sure that he and all those
listening recognised the appalling implications of what we
had just heard.

THE COURT: Please listen carefully to my questions. As
I understand it, it's not pleasant for you to come to
this court in the presence of numerous people, and the
media, numerous people in the audience . . .

A: That's correct.

THE COURT: . . . and disclose portions of your life.

A: That's correct.

THE COURT: And you didn't want to testify in court?

A: That's correct.

THE COURT: And you so indicated to the District Attorney's Office on several occasions?

A: Yes.

THE COURT: Now, there were times when the District Attorney's Office called you and asked you to come down, and wanted you to come down, and you hung up on them?

A: Yes.

THE COURT: And they kept calling you. They just didn't give up?

A: Right.

THE COURT: You also say that the District Attorneys you saw called you names?

A: Yes.

THE COURT: What names did they call you?

A: They didn't call me names that are going to be derogatory. They said things like a mischievous child, or that the interpretation of this case if I did not come to trial would be that I was basically a liar. That's not a direct quote, but that's the gist.

THE COURT: The thrust of what they said was that?

A: Yes. Yes.

THE COURT: And they said that to you not once but several times?

A: Yes. Yes.

THE COURT: And using your phraseology you were not anxious to expose yourself to the public in respect of this matter?

A: Sure. Yes.

THE COURT: And they told you that – finally, that you had to come?

A: Yes.

THE COURT: Were you in any way reluctant with respect to testifying before the Grand Jury?

A: Yes, but I did appear before them.

THE COURT: As reluctant as you were when you wrote that letter?

A: Yes.

THE COURT: You were just as reluctant to go to non-jury?

A: No, I – my answer is no to that because the Grand Jury was supposed – the cases – I was told that the cases usually can go to the Grand Jury and that the defendant will take a plea from the Grand Jury case.
THE COURT: You did appear, though?
A: Yes.
THE COURT: Go ahead.

The rest of that session was spent by Mr Kennedy establishing that John Schaefer now felt anger and resentment towards me, and that he believed I should be punished, feelings he admitted he had not felt before he had spoken to FBI Agent McDonald. By now John was getting very flustered and his cockiness had deserted him. He kept darting glances towards the Prosecution table, almost imploring the D.A. to help him. He looked very young and vulnerable, foundering in the mess of his own lies. Finally, he was forced to request a brief recess to compose himself, and this was granted without objection from my attorney.

Chapter
Fourteen

One would have thought it impossible that anything funny would happen in a court where such serious charges were being tried. But there was one incident which was then, and still is, as I recall it, hilarious. It concerned the picture of Aphrodite which John had seen in the hallway of my apartment and had described as an indication of my supposed depravity. Mr Kennedy decided to ask him about this.

Q: Mr Schaefer, you told us in direct examination that on two occasions you've been to Father Lynch's apartment, is that correct?
A: Yes.
Q: And so, on two occasions you saw this picture of
– who was it?
A: Hermaphrodite.
Q: Of Hermaphrodite?
A: Yes.
Q: And this picture had – it was surrounded by some netting, was it?
A: Yes.
Q: And had a young woman with a breast exposed?
A: Yes.
Q: Who had a penis?

A: I could tell there was a penis there, yes.
Q: You're sure of that?
A: I'm almost positive, yes.
Q: Thank you.

Mr Kennedy asked that two neighbours of mine, middle-aged ladies, be allowed to bring the picture into court. The two women triumphantly marched down the aisle carrying this huge picture – 3^1/$_2$ feet by 2^1/$_2$ feet – draped in a white sheet. With great gusto Mr Kennedy did the unveiling, standing about twelve feet from the Judge and John Schaefer.

Q: Mr Schaefer, is that the picture?
A: Yes.
Q: Would you show his Honor where the penis is on the picture of this young woman?
A: There isn't a penis there.
Q: There is not?
A: No.
Q: So that's another – mistake, is it?
A: Yes.
Q: You see penises where they don't exist, John Schaefer, is that the truth?
A: No, I'm sure it came from a suggestion, sir.
Q: Oh. I see. Now, you described that picture as a picture of Hermaphrodite, did you not?
A: Yes, I did.
Q: Actually, if you look at it –
A: Young Aphrodite.
Q: So, it's Aphrodite, isn't it?
A: Yes.
Q: You know the difference between Hermaphrodite and Aphrodite?
A: Yes, I do. But let me – you want to know where I learned, it was when I was shown this picture –
THE COURT: When you were shown –
A: Yes. It was – I had never heard – I had never heard

118

the term before I was in his apartment that day, and when we came to the picture, then it was described as Hermaphrodite, and that's why it sticks in my mind and I thought it said Hermaphrodite on it.

Q: This is the same picture?

A: Yes.

Q: And you were convinced that – you were convinced that you thought you saw a penis in that picture?

A: Yes.

Q: But there isn't any penis in the picture?

A: Penis in the picture, correct.

Q: That's another mistake, isn't it?

A: Yes.

Q: And you hoped the first mistake I found would be the last one?

A: Yes, I did.

Q: You were sure it would be?

A: Yes, I was, and I was wrong.

Q: Now I found another mistake?

A: I was wrong.

Q. Quite.

Mr Kennedy moved on to the contents of the complaint John Schaefer had lodged against me, asking him to read directly from the complaint as issued under oath.

A: 'That the defendant's said conduct has caused the plaintiff great pain, humiliation, embarrassment, severe emotional reaction and distress, invoking suicidal ideation in the plaintiff, and otherwise causing great sorrow and grief and required that the plaintiff seek therapy in an effort to relieve himself of same.'

Q: And the defendant you're referring to who did all those terrible things to you is none other than Father Bernard Lynch, is that correct?

A: That's correct.

Q: Would it be fair to say that you were troubled

by the confusion you had about your own sexual identity?

A: Yes.

Q: And that was among the things you brought to the attention of Father Lynch, was it not?

A: Yes.

Q: And Father Lynch would keep saying to you — well, you should seek additional guidance, additional therapy, additional counseling, correct?

A: Yes.

Q: But you never did?

A: No.

Q: Do you remember Brother Tom Long?

A: Yes.

Q: From Mount St Michael's?

A: Yes.

Q: He was a guidance counselor, wasn't he?

A: Yes.

Q: So Mount St Michael's had a formal counsel structure of some sort, did they not?

A: Yes.

Q: And a woman called Mary Catherine Freeman also participated in that, didn't she?

A: Yes she did.

Q: So, Father Lynch wasn't technically a counselor, he was technically the campus chaplain?

A: Yes.

Q: But when you would seek counseling you wouldn't go to the guidance counselor, you would go to Father Lynch?

A: That's correct.

Q: Because you found Father Lynch more sympathetic, fair?

A: I don't — that would not be my choice of words, no.

Q: What would be your choice of words?

A: Easiest to talk to.

Q: Easier to talk to, more understanding?

A: Yes.

Q: More tolerant?

A: Yes.

Q: Someone you could trust?

A: Yes.

Q: Someone you could confide in and rely on him to protect your various confidences?

A: Yes.

Q: Okay. You found him a caring person?

A: Yes.

Q: And you found him a tolerant person?

A: Yes.

Q: Not the sort of person who would impose his views on another person, correct?

A: No.

Q: So prior to this alleged incident where you accuse him of sexually molesting you, you found Father Lynch to be a caring, tolerant person?

A: Yes.

Q: Someone who was opposed to violence?

A: Yes.

Q: Someone who says the way to solve problems is to talk them out?

A: Yes.

Q: Not someone who might take advantage of power, was he?

A: No.

Q: Not someone who would deliberately hurt someone, was he?

A: No.

Q: Not someone you were at all afraid of?

A: No.

Q: You were attracted to Father Lynch, were you not?

A: No, I wasn't.

Q: I mean you were drawn to him. I didn't mean you were hot for him.

A: I'm glad you verified that.

Q: He was someone who had your trust and your confidence?

A: Yes.

Q: You enjoyed seeing him?

A: Yes.

Q: Enjoyed being with him?

A: Yes.

Q: Enjoyed talking to him?

A: Yes.

Q: You even enjoyed the light banter that you would have with him?

A: Yes.

Q: The jokes?

A: Yes.

Q: And you knew when you were joking you were joking, and when you were serious you were serious?

A: Yes.

Q: And when Father Lynch would make a joke to you, would you think he was coming on to you physically, sexually?

A: No.

Q: Didn't you say to Agent McDonald that you thought prior to the incident that you thought Father Lynch was coming on to you regularly.

A: In retrospect, yes. See, that's why I'm clarifying. At the time of the incident happening I did not think anything of them. In retrospect after the fact, yes, I thought something of them.

Q: So, at the time of these so-called comings on sexually, you didn't think he was coming on to you sexually?

A: Correct.

Q: Only when you sit down with an FBI agent do you look back on them and say, ah-ha, he was coming on to me sexually?

This line of questioning continued, amid many objections

from the Prosecution, for over an hour. It became more
and more obvious that what John Schaefer had told Agent
McDonald was said only after the insinuation of misconduct
had been placed in his disturbed mind by Agent McDonald
himself. Mr Kennedy then broached the subject that was to
prove the most damning to the prosecution case.

Q: If you thought Father Lynch was serious about his
comings on, you would never, John Schaefer, have gone
to his apartment alone, would you?
A: That's correct.
Q: And what was the reason you went to his apart-
ment?
A: I went there for a project in school.
Q: What was that project?
A: A psychology paper.
Q: Because you were taking a psychology course at New
Rochelle Academy?
A: Yes I was.
Q: That was a course taught by Mr Field, was it?
A: Yes.
Q: Mr Field gave an assignment to you to interview,
to do some field work?
A: Right.
Q: To interview a counselor?
A: Correct.
Q: And you chose the man?
A: Yes.
Q: Father Lynch, correct?
A: Yes.
Q: And you're certain – quite certain – that was in
January of 1985?
A: Yes.
Q: Okay. Isn't it possible that in *1986* you took a psy-
chology course for the first time, and not in 1985?
A: I was sitting in on a class in 1985. If you look at
my record at New Rochelle Academy you'll see I went

there as a second semester freshman. I attended that school for a year and a half. I graduated in 1986.

Q: Let's look at your transcript then, Mr Schaefer. Please tell his Honor whether or not you can identify it.

A: Yes I can. It's my transcript from New Rochelle Academy.

MR WALSH: Objection.

THE COURT: What's the objection?

MR WALSH: I ask for an offer of proof why he's putting in the person's entire academic record in school. Basically this is a privileged document. There is no reason to put it in unless there is a specific thing he wants.

THE COURT: What do you want specifically, Mr Kennedy?

MR KENNEDY: He doesn't take psychology until 1986.

THE COURT: For that limited purpose –

MR WALSH: He answered that.

MR KENNEDY: He's not telling the truth. I am entitled to demonstrate that. I want the whole document in.

THE COURT: What's the purpose of that?

MR KENNEDY: Because he's not going to be able to weasel out the way he is when the document is in front of him. He's now in a desperate situation. He says the only reason he goes to Father Lynch's apartment in January, 1985 is because he needs to work on a psychology paper. I will prove that the psychology paper was taken the following year, that he came to Bernard Lynch's apartment a year after the alleged event and asked him to help him with the psychology paper. And that's just not how you treat someone who has just molested you.

MR WALSH: He already gave the explanation that he sat in on the course the year before.

MR KENNEDY: You don't get work assignments when you sit in.

THE COURT: Your objection is overruled.

Q: You previously identified that as a transcript from New Rochelle Academy, did you not, Mr Schaefer?

A: That's correct.

Q: It indicates that you took a psychology course, does it not?

A: Yes.

Q: And it indicates that you got credit for that psychology course in the year 1986, correct?

A: That's correct.

Q: Now, it is a fact, is it not, that you went to see Father Lynch to do work on a paper for a psychology course at New Rochelle Academy — that's a fact, isn't it?

A: Yes.

Q: What I'm suggesting to you is that you're wrong about the dates: that happened in 1986 and not in 1985, Mr Schaefer. And that's what this document reflects, doesn't it?

A: Yes, it does.

Q: It also reflects the actual course you took in 1985, doesn't it?

A: Yes, it does.

Q: And there's no psychology course listed in 1985 for you, is there?

A: No.

Q: You've no reason to believe that New Rochelle Academy made a mistake in the preparation of your transcript, do you?

A: No.

Q: All right. Does it refresh your recollection, Mr Schaefer, that it was in fact in 1986 that you were taking a psychology course, the same course that caused you to seek the counsel of Father Lynch?

A: Your Honor — is there any way —

Q: Answer the question first.

A: Is there any way I may speak to my lawyer?

THE COURT: Do you have any objection to him conferring with the Assistant D.A.?

MR KENNEDY: Yes. I certainly do.

THE COURT: Then I will not permit it.

MR KENNEDY: I would like the benefit of his testimony untutored by my very wise colleague, Mr Walsh.

THE COURT: Let me ask you this, Mr Schaefer. You recall seeing Father Lynch in 1985, is that correct?

A: Yes.

THE COURT: At that time you were not taking any psychology course for credit?

A: That's correct.

THE COURT: But you state that in 1985 you were sitting in on a psychology course?

A: You could sit in on any course.

THE COURT: When you sit in on a course you don't take exams in that course, do you?

A: No, but you're permitted to do work because that course is offered.

THE COURT: Let me ask the question. Don't anticipate what I might ask. I might not have asked you that question. You don't take exams?

A: No.

THE COURT: You could read the textbook if you got a textbook?

A: Sure.

THE COURT: You wouldn't have to turn in a paper for a course you were just sitting in on, would you?

A: No.

THE COURT: But it is your testimony that during 1985 you were sitting in on a course, and without obtaining any credit for it you decided on your own to take an assignment which was given to the class?

A: Correct.

THE COURT: And follow through on that assignment?

A: Correct.

THE COURT: Was the paper then going to be given to the teacher for marking?

A: I believe I would have kept it for the following year, your Honor.

THE COURT: In other words you state that in 1985,

when you were sitting in on a course, you decided to go along with an assignment which the teacher gave to the class, and then hold the results of your assignment until the following year and utilize it when you took the psychology course for credit the following year?

A: Correct.

THE COURT: Now is it altogether possible that all of this occurred when you were taking the psychology course for credit?

A: It is possible, your Honor. I can't say under oath that it is not possible.

THE COURT: You say it is possible.

A: Yes.

THE COURT: Now, if *that's* possible, then it is possible that this event occurred in 1986 as opposed to 1985, is that correct?

A: Correct.

THE COURT: You're not certain of that?

A: I'm not certain. No.

THE COURT: Go ahead, Mr Kennedy.

Q: Do you recall testifying to the Grand Jury that 'I got a project from my psycho-professor in high school. I needed to interview a counselor for a paper I had to do. I called from my girlfriend's house in Riverdale because Father Lynch only lived down the block.' Do you recall that testimony?

A: Yes, I do.

Q: But now it is *possible*, is it not, that, in fact, the meeting with Father Lynch on the psychology paper did not occur in January of 1985, but, in fact, occurred in 1986 when you were taking the psychology course?

A: It is possible. I'm not saying that it happened, I'm — I just —

Q: And if *that's* possible, that means that a year after you say Father Lynch forcibly molested you, you call him up and go to his apartment alone in the evening to see him to get help on a psychology paper, correct?

127

A: No, the two events are related, sir.

Q: If your recollection about the incident where you accuse Father Lynch of molesting you was at the same time as you were seeking his assistance on a psychology paper – that is your recollection, isn't it?

A: Yes.

Q: Then it is possible, is it not, that that alleged molestation occurred in 1986 and not in 1985?

A: The two events happened together.

Q: So it is possible?

A: Yes. Yes.

Q: So it is possible that you are mistaken by a whole year as to when this alleged molestation took place, correct?

A: Correct.

Q: All right. On that note, your Honor, I think we can adjourn this evening and pick up again tomorrow morning.

THE COURT: All right. How much longer will you be on cross-examination, do you know?

MR KENNEDY: I would venture half an hour.

THE COURT: All right. This matter will be recessed until tomorrow at 11 o'clock.

Needless to say, the media had a field-day. Even to these self-confessed cynics it was becoming clear that there was more behind this trial than just some dirty old man caught with his hand down a boy's pants. They recognised that I had been set up, and they were beginning to want to know why.

Chapter
Fifteen

The morning session on the following day was taken up mostly with what is called 'Proceedings'. That is when both attorneys confer with the Judge at the bench. Judge Roberts appreciated the significance of John Schaefer's confusion about the dates and was determined that the matter be clarified in the best way possible despite the Prosecution's attempts to blur the matter.

Judge Roberts therefore decided to question John Schaefer himself, giving the young man every opportunity to be more precise about his testimony. He led him through the events again, seeking some means whereby John could be more exact. What about the girlfriend he had been visiting the evening he came to my apartment? When had he met up with her? Could she not help establish the year? What about his teacher, Mr Field? Could he help?

John Schaefer was given the exceptional privilege of being allowed to leave the court and telephone both these people to establish for the court which year, in fact, was the true one. Neither of these, it seemed, could help.

Other inconsistencies were now coming to light. John had stated that on the night in question he had only been in my apartment for twenty minutes, but he now told the Judge that he had been there for an hour, 'give or take a few minutes'.

THE COURT: Your testimony is that you were in the apartment for about an hour, which would include the interview and the alleged incident, is that what you're saying now?

A: Yes. Yes.

THE COURT: So you were not there for just twenty minutes?

A: No I was there – No. No. Just twenty minutes.

It also came to light that the psychology paper was something of a red herring.

Q: For example, you never said to FBI Agent McDonald anything about a psychology paper, did you?

A: No, I did not.

Q: The first time you mentioned the psychology paper was in front of the Grand Jury, correct?

A: That's correct, after being prepped by the D.A.'s Office.

Q: Ah-ha. And that preparation by the District Attorney's Office was by the then Assistant District Attorney, Mitch Garber?

A: And A.D.A. Jennings.

Q: And after the incident of Father Lynch and the psychology paper, did you ever take those notes and put them in any form that might be appropriate to submit them to a teacher?

A: No I did not.

Q: What did you do with them?

A: I don't know. It could be a notebook I've thrown out. I don't know. I don't know.

What was astonishing was that the D.A.'s Office had made such a poor job of coaching their witness. It is possible they did not realise just how suggestible and vulnerable John was.

Q: Now, when you filed a verified civil complaint in this case, you made reference, did you not, under oath, to the psychology paper that you had to write, did you not?

A: Yes.

Q: Please read Paragraph 11 aloud for his Honor.

A: 'That on Friday night between January 1, 1985 and February 1, 1985, Plaintiff called Defendant at home and asked if he could discuss a paper assigned to him at his then present school which –'

Q: So, under oath you're saying you were assigned a paper, correct?

A: Which involved interviewing a psychologist or counselor.

Q: And that assignment came from a teacher?

A: Which involved interviewing a psychologist or counselor, yes.

Q: Normally, when one gets an assignment the teacher expects us to come back with something, correct?

A: That's correct.

Q: But in this case, you're saying, your teacher didn't expect you to come back with this assignment, is that what you're saying?

The questioning moved on to the subject of my sobriety.

Q: Now, as I understood your testimony, you said under oath yesterday that Father Lynch, on that occasion, when you accuse him of having molested you, offered you a glass of wine. Do you recall that?

A: Yes.

Q: When asked the same question in front of the Grand Jury, do you recall what you told the Grand Jury?

A: No I don't.

Q: Well, maybe I can refresh your recollection. Please read what you said.

MR WALSH: Objection.

THE COURT: Sustained.

Q: Does it refresh your recollection as to what you said in front of the Grand Jury?

A: Yes, it does.

Q: And it does not say you were offered a glass of wine, does it?

A: No.

Q: What does it say you were offered?

A: I had something to drink – soda or juice.

Q: Soda or juice. Yes. Now, you also testified yesterday that on that occasion Father Lynch was unlike you had ever seen him before. Do you recall saying that?

A: Yes.

Q: He was very unusual, you thought, maybe he was even intoxicated?

A: Possibly.

Q: Were you asked, in the same context, by the Grand Jury this question: 'What happened when you went to the apartment?' Were you asked that question?

A: Yes.

Q: And did you give the answer: 'He let me in. I had a soda or something to drink, soda or juice. We were just talking. He was his usual self.' Did you give that answer?

A: Yes, I did.

Q: Under oath?

A: Yes.

Q: Trying to be truthful to the Grand Jury?

A: Yes.

Q: Were you, then, trying to deceive his Honor yesterday when you said he was acting utterly unusual?

MR WALSH: Objection.

A: No I wasn't.

Slowly, inexorably, John Schaefer was being shown as a person who made totally contradictory statements, under oath, on separate occasions.

Q: Now, you visited a psychotherapist, Jeanette Golden, for about five visits in 1988. Do you recall that?
A: Yes.
Q: Do you also recall talking to her about your home and family life?
A: Yes.
Q: Did you tell her that your mother was an alcoholic?
A: No I did not.
Q: So Jeanette Golden – when it says in Jeanette Golden's records that you said your mother was an alcoholic, Jeanette Golden is mistaken? Did you tell her that your stepfather was an abusive person?
A: No I did not.

But not only was John apparently unable to differentiate fact from imagination; he exhibited, in my view and in that of others, a belief in a strange fantasy world in which he played a leading role. Some of his cockiness returned when it was revealed that there was a standing joke about him being German from the waist up, and Italian from the waist down.

Q: Being Italian from the waist down had to do with the large size of your penis as part of the joke, wasn't it?
A: I think being Italian from the waist down meant a lot of things.
Q: Was that among them?
A: People could think that if they wanted.
Q: That's what you thought it meant?
A: I thought it meant that I was a stud or something.
Q: Well-endowed might be another way.
A: No, I'm saying I was a stud.

For the final part of his cross-examination Mr Kennedy

concentrated on the strange behaviour of John Schaefer towards myself, someone who had supposedly molested him against his will.

Q: Now, after the incident, wherein you accused Father Lynch of having abused you, you called Father Lynch and asked him to officiate at the funeral Mass of your grandmother, correct?
A: Yes.
Q: Father Lynch says, 'I'm sorry, I cannot because of another commitment,' correct?
A: That's correct.
Q: But indicates that he will come and attend the wake, correct?
A: That's correct.
Q: And he did attend the wake of your grandmother?
A: Yes, he did.
Q: And you saw him there?
A: Yes.
Q: And you greeted him?
A: Yes.
Q: Did you embrace?
A: Yes.
Q: And you acted for all the world as though nothing had ever happened between you and Father Lynch, didn't you?
A: Yes.
Q: Okay. Then in December 1986, your mother gave birth?
A: In October.
Q: In October to a girl child?
A: Correct.
Q: Named Ashley, am I correct?
A: Yes.
Q: And Ashley was to be baptized or christened?
A: Correct.
Q: In December 1986, do you recall calling Father Lynch

and asking him if he would officiate as the priest at the christening of your stepsister?

A: Half-sister, yes.

Q: And he accepted, did he not?

A: Yes.

Q: And indeed, on the 18th day of January, 1987, Father Lynch baptized your half-sister, Ashley?

A: That's correct.

Q: And after the baptism service at the church there was a reception?

A: Yes.

Q: A bit of a party?

A: Yes.

Q: Father Lynch came to the reception?

A: Yes.

Q: You saw him there?

A: Yes.

Q: You were friendly?

A: Yes.

Q: He even held your half-sister?

A: I believe he did, yes.

Q: And you acted for all the world, did you not, Mr Schaefer, as though nothing untoward, nothing bad had ever happened between you and Father Lynch, didn't you?

A: Yes.

Q: You wanted the entire world to believe that you and Father Lynch were still close, correct?

A: Yes.

Q: And that was the last time you saw him, wasn't it?

A: Yes.

Q: But you've spoken to him on the phone since then, haven't you?

A: I believe so.

Q: Now, you didn't tell the FBI or the Grand Jury anything about Father Lynch coming to your grandmother's wake, did you?

A: I don't believe so, no.

Q: Now, in November of '87, do you recall making a telephone call to the number you had for Bernard Lynch and receiving a recorded message on an answering machine?

A: It's possible, but I don't remember.

THE COURT: This would be after you spoke to Agent McDonald?

A: I spoke to Father Lynch one more time, but I don't know – I don't remember who called who.

Q: Would it refresh your recollection if I suggested to you that you called Father Lynch around November of '87, and got an answering machine, and left a number where Father Lynch could reach you?

A: That's possible.

Q: Does the number, Area Code 516 243–1436 – is that a number with which you are familiar?

A: Yes.

Q: That was a telephone number of yours, was it not?

A: Yes.

Q: Do you recall now Father Lynch called you on that number?

A: Like I said, I spoke to him one time after that. So it's possible.

Q: But he did call you at that number?

A: I'm saying I spoke to him one more time.

Q: You mentioned to the FBI when you came to testify to the Grand Jury that you had gotten an *unexpected* call from Father Lynch on an unlisted number, didn't you?

A: It was an unlisted number, yes, and yes, it was unexpected.

Q: But didn't you leave the number on the answering machine for Father Lynch?

A: I don't remember.

Q: You could have?

A: I don't remember.

THE COURT: If I may. After you had spoken to Agent McDonald and after this investigation had begun where you went to the District Attorney's office, and saw Mitch Garber, what would be, if you could recall, the purpose of your calling Father Lynch?

A: I don't know your Honor.

THE COURT: You have no recollection whatsoever?

A: I don't remember making the phone call, but – there were a lot of times I wanted to call him and tell him what I did say to the D.A., but I never did.

THE COURT: Did you speak to him?

A: I spoke to him one time after.

THE COURT: What, if anything, did you say to him, and what did he say to you in that particular conversation?

A: I don't remember. I think it was very general. I did not tell him about the case. We just talked –

THE COURT: You did not discuss the case at all?

A: No.

THE COURT: He didn't ask you any questions about the case and you didn't volunteer any information about the case?

A: No.

THE COURT: Proceed, Mr Kennedy.

MR KENNEDY: I have no further questions, your Honor.

Judge Roberts was none too satisfied with the witness. He was clearly bemused by the fact that John Schaefer could not give a satisfactory date, not even the year, of the incident in which I was accused of being involved. From the bench he questioned John Schaefer himself, trying to establish once and for all when the supposed molestation took place:

THE COURT: Before we proceed with redirect . . . You have testified with respect to the dates or the date that this incident occurred. You have indicated that it is now your best recollection, and it is your testimony that it

137

did *not* occur between January 1, 1985 and January 31, 1985, is that correct?

A: That's correct.

THE COURT: This particular time, after speaking to the teacher of the psychology course on the telephone this morning and after speaking to the young woman whom you say you were dating at that particular time, after talking about the fact that you saw that young woman before you went up to see Father Lynch, and after stating at that particular juncture it was a time when you believe the young woman was reciprocating a gift you had given her for her birthday and it was either Christmas or Hanukkah – she being Jewish –

A: I believe it was, like, mid-December, like, the second week of December.

THE COURT: Like somewhere between the 4th and the 24th of December certainly.

A: Yes.

THE COURT: All right. Having that information, and further stating that it was cold weather, can you approximate, on or about, using whatever scope you wish to make – and see if you can narrow it as far as possible – can you state when this occurred, on or about, or what date?

A: The only thing I can say is I know it now occurred during my senior year of High School which was September of '85 to June of '86.

THE COURT: You know it did not occur in '85, it occurred sometime after September of '86, and it occurred sometime when it was cold outside?

A: Sometime after September '85.

THE COURT: After September of '85?

A: Right.

THE COURT: And the weather was cold?

A: Yes.

THE COURT: And it occurred after a time you had visited your girlfriend?

A: Correct.

THE COURT: Can you give us an approximation of the date, recognizing that it was cold weather, or you say it was cold weather, can you give us any approximation of the date at all?

A: I can't, your Honor.

THE COURT: You cannot?

A: No.

THE COURT: So, at this particular juncture, all we know is that it wasn't in '85, and you can't pinpoint a date. Can you give us a year?

A: Possibly '85, because September of '85 –

THE COURT: So it would be from September of '85 through what month?

A: Through March of '86.

THE COURT: So, the date of this incident is anywhere from September of '85 through March of '86? That's as close as you can pinpoint?

A: Yes.

THE COURT: And you eliminate January 1 to January 31, 1985?

A: Yes.

THE COURT: And what we have now is September 1, 1985 through March 31, 1986, as being one of the dates in that particular time interval as being the date in which you went to visit Father Lynch, is that correct?

A: Yes.

THE COURT: And where the alleged incident occurred?

A: Yes.

THE COURT: All right. You may proceed with redirect.

The Prosecution requested another recess: 'I would like time to prepare the redirect for this witness. It's now five o'clock. I would like to get hold of the transcript. There are many things I'd like to go over with this witness. Besides, it's been a long cross-examination, over several days. I'd like

139

to recess, resume tomorrow, and I believe we could finish
redirect rather quickly at that point.'

Judge Roberts did not look happy. All of John Schaefer's
evidence had indicated a climate of collusion and coaching
in an effort to make a case against me, when in fact there
was no case. 'You can't do it today?'

'I think, your Honour, this witness has indicated that he
wished to speak to me,' Mr Walsh replied.

'I said I'd permit you to speak to him now. I permit you
to give him half an hour recess to speak to him.'

'Your Honour, I would like to sit down with him, go
through everything. I would like him to be relaxed, and
to ask him to start redirect at six o'clock I don't think is
reasonable. I would simply ask the case go over to tomorrow,
give him an opportunity to sleep on it, have an opportunity
to go through these issues and resolve them tomorrow. I
don't think we would lose that much time.'

'Is this going to be the People's case as a result of this
witness, or are you going to call additional witnesses?'

'That would be one of the things that I would determine
in speaking to the witness.'

'But you certainly expect to finish the People's case by
noontime tomorrow?'

'I will try. Certainly it will be my hope to finish the
case.'

'All right. Anything else? Have a good evening.'

It seemed to me and to my attorneys that the Federal agents
would continue to do what they had done previously: taking
John Schaefer aside to work on his story, and to push him
to continue. The more stupid it looked, the less it mattered.
This evening, before the last day of the trial, I said to myself,
They're too powerful, I can't win.

Chapter
Sixteen

The events of the following day in court were described by Bob Teague as 'mind-boggling'. In fairness to everyone I will quote them in full from the official court transcript, dated April 21, 1989, Indictment No. 2627/88. Justice Burton Roberts began, addressing himself to the prosecuting lawyer, Assistant District Attorney Mr Sean Walsh: 'When we recessed yesterday afternoon we were going to commence with the redirect. Are you ready to proceed?'

MR WALSH: Your Honor, at this time the People have an application. The People wish to adjourn this case until Monday morning for several reasons. I spoke to John Schaefer yesterday evening and discussed redirect with him. We further discussed the dates and other details. With respect to that he has put together some thoughts of his own. There are some further matters that must be clarified to assure accurate testimony, and second of all, the most important of all, in speaking to him this morning I don't think he is ready, emotionally, to return to the stand and deal with this. Obviously and very clearly, he had difficulties on cross-examination. He has a great deal of difficulty with these dates. He's concerned about testifying very accurately, fairly, honestly. To put this witness on the stand at this time in his state of mind would not be fair to him nor to the defendant nor to the interests of justice. I know this case has tended to drag in the last several days. I think in the interest of fairness to all parties in this case if we could resolve this matter with a degree of accuracy and fairness, the interest of justice would be better met by this adjournment until Monday, and I think that would best serve the interest of the Court and the defendant as well as the witness.

MR KENNEDY: Your Honor, to the extent that they're trying to get Mr Schaefer to perfect his testimony, in my view that's a waste of time. Your Honor, I think, exhausted those possibilities yesterday and the day before, and I attempted my own way also. With all due respect to the counsel, I'm not sure he's in a position to evaluate this young man. I would ask the Court to bring Mr Schaefer in. You're the fact-finder and if you feel that he's not in a state to continue then that's another matter, but if it's over the evidence, if it's over the facts, if it's over the time, that seems to me to be beside the point.

THE COURT: Let me just state for the record, now, as Judge in this case that I have found Mr Schaefer perfectly capable of answering questions with regard to the incident which has occurred. The only problem that has arisen with respect to the testimony deals with the setting of dates as to when this last occurred. When I questioned him yesterday afternoon I was able to ascertain the following: we were able to ascertain that the events occurred between September when he began school and March 31. Further, we discovered that at the time that this occurred he was seeing this young woman. There was some discussion with respect to a reciprocal gift given to him either during Christmas — for Christmas or for Hanukkah. There was a discussion with regard to that.

I would certainly think that some time frame could be obtained, particularly with respect to a situation in which it is the contention of the Defense that, indeed, there was a visit by this young man on two occasions to the home of Father Lynch. The contention of the Defense as to what transpired during those visits is different from the contention of the People and the State and testimony of the witness. There were plenty of breaks yesterday with respect to cross-examination in this case. This case should be treated like any other case, and certainly great leeway has been given with respect to this witness who was able to leave the stand for a considerable length of time to telephone his teacher and check with him. That proved unavailing. He also spoke to this young girl who was his girlfriend at the time. I do not know whether that provided him with a freshener with respect to his recollection, but you were invited to speak to him at any time. I do not see what is to be gained by prolonging this. There is a witness on the stand. Certain allegations have been made. I would think that we should proceed with this matter, and I would now direct he be ready to proceed with this trial at 2.15.

MR WALSH: Your Honor, please, you said several things there that I would like to comment on – respond to. You said that this is like any other trial. It is not like any other trial. As we all know the case involves sexual abuse. These are very sensitive cases, very difficult cases for people to talk about, to discuss. Very emotional cases. There's a great deal of concern. Your Honor's effort to resolve these problems yesterday by letting him leave the stand so often to clarify something was, in my opinion, not the best way to do so. It just created more problems in the end by checking individual points. The problem is not perfecting a date. I have an obligation of presenting evidence to this Court that I'm satisfied with and confident that the testimony of this witness is going to be correct. I'm not concerned with the date

143

or the time. He can testify to that. What I'm concerned about is this witness being able to testify accurately and honestly, and under an emotional situation I must feel he'll give the best answers in the court as he can recollect. It's my opinion that he cannot at this time. I've discussed this with him and I'm concerned –

THE COURT: I direct that he be brought up forthwith and placed on the witness stand. I will speak to him. When we talk about child abuse cases we are dealing with sexual abuse cases where we are dealing with four- and five-year-old children. This individual is a graduate of high school. He is eighteen or nineteen years of age. There are many people of eighteen or nineteen years of age that are mature enough to do quite a bit more than testify on a witness stand.

MR WALSH: Some do and some don't. That's the issue.

THE COURT: This Court did at that particular age, and I think being able to testify on a witness stand is not so monumental or should create such an emotional disturbance. I will talk to the young man, and I'm sure we will be able to proceed.

MR WALSH: Call him now?

THE COURT: Please . . . Will someone give Mr Schaefer a glass of water? How do you feel this morning?

A: I've been better, your Honor.

THE COURT: You have now been on the stand for a couple of days. My first word of advice to you with respect to your well-being is that you get on the stand to testify, and when you go home do not turn on any television set because what you see on television with regard to this case really has nothing to do with what this Court is going to do in deciding this case. Things that are stated on television are extraneous, are not within the gamut of the evidence that I have to consider, and I have made it a practice that as soon as something is on television about this case I walk out. I have heard the defendant and the Defense counsel go on television

which is their right. It is my duty to walk away from it.
I am sure you have been watching it. You should not be
watching it because it has nothing to do with this case.
What we have to consider here is the evidence, which is
the testimony that you gave, and answers to questions.
I do not care what goes on outside the courtroom. I'm
interested only in the evidence in this particular case.
Do you understand what I'm saying?

A: Yes, your Honor.

THE COURT: So, if I assure you – in case that gives you
any feeling of unrest with regard to the testimony that
you gave – that you are just on the stand to answer
questions to the best of your ability, and you are here
to let the chips fall where they may even if they hurt or
help the People's case, or hurt or help the defendant's
case, do you understand that?

A: Yes, your Honor.

THE COURT: I have not noticed you in any distress up
there. You have been answering questions relative to
the case.

A: Yes, your Honor. I haven't been here for a twenty-
four-hour period. There's a lot of things people don't
hear. There's a lot of things the family sees. There's a
lot of things the D.A.'s Office has seen.

THE COURT: What I'm telling you now is this: all I'm
interested in – and I am the trier of the facts – is the
testimony as the evidence which is adduced during the
course of this trial, so do not worry about what anyone
else sees. The media have a perfect right to cover the
story the way they wish.

A: I understand that, your Honor.

THE COURT: They are interested in news. I am interested
in the legal evidence which is adduced during the course
of this trial, and you just relax, sit back there. Take a
drink of water and we'll finish your testimony today.

A: I just want to say one thing. I feel emotionally – and
to be fair to the defendant and to be fair to everybody

145

here – that my testimony has been – has been amended, and I'm trying to get to the bottom of everything. I feel emotionally in the past two days – they have been very, very straining on myself, and I feel to give the best testimony I'll need some time to recoup. I don't know if I can give an accurate description of – of all the events, of the dates and such. I'm trying to as best I can –

THE COURT: What I'm interested in here is the events that transpired. With respect to the date you will have a lunch hour to sit down with counsel and dig into that date, if you will. We have already indicated that there are certain things you have already testified to concerning that date. You have indicated now that it occurred when you went to psychology class. You indicated when you were dating this young woman. You indicated that you met this young woman some time – was it in January of –

A: Of '85.

THE COURT: '85, and you believe it was when the weather was cold, correct?

A: Yes, your Honor, but I have reason to believe that some of that may be amended as well. I don't feel that right now I'm ready to go forward and discuss –

THE COURT: Then you will sit down during the lunch hour and talk it out with your counsel. You can only do the best you can with regard to the events that transpired according to your best recollection some time – in view of your last testimony – between September '85 and March of '86.

A: I have reason to believe that may not be the date, your Honor.

THE COURT: Then you will testify to the best of your ability as to what the date is, and I will listen to your testimony. I will hear your explanation and I will evaluate the evidence as best I am able.

Let us proceed. If you want to leave off the date at

this particular time or discuss the date, we can go into other redirect. If you would prefer, Mr Walsh, during the lunch hour, to sit down with him for the next hour in order to ascertain the date, we will see where we are going.

MR WALSH: It's up to the witness, your Honor. I've already discussed the date.

THE COURT: Do you wish to proceed now or do you want to sit down with him for an hour at lunch before you begin your testimony?

A: I'm under the opinion that all of these facts are represented and related to the date. I don't know if I can give an accurate testimony on anything until I have some further time to speak with my counsel.

THE COURT: Then you will have it. I will give you that hour, and that is what you are going to have. And after that hour you are going to go on this stand and you will answer questions. Do I make myself clear?

A: Yes, your Honor.

THE COURT: I will give you that hour and then you will get on the stand and answer questions posed by both sides.

A: Yes, your Honor.

THE COURT: Do you understand what I'm saying?

A: Yes.

THE COURT: Your testimony will be completed today. We will recess now until two thirty ... two thirty-five. I will give you exactly an hour. Two thirty-five.

The court reconvened promptly at two thirty-five. The afternoon session brought an immediate sensation.

THE COURT: Mr Walsh?

MR WALSH: Yes, sir. Mr Schaefer –

THE COURT: Call Mr Schaefer.

MR WALSH: The People are not calling Mr Schaefer at

this time. Your Honor, at this time the People have a statement to make for court.

THE COURT: Fine.

MR WALSH: During the luncheon recess I spoke to Mr Schaefer. I also spoke to a counselor who has been dealing with him from our office. Mr Schaefer became physically sick during lunch. He was unable to finish his lunch. In fact, he threw it up. My colleague who is assisting me in this case has spoken to a doctor who is working for our office who advises us in these matters. It's based on her professional opinion that this witness, from what we've told her and what she's actually seen in news reports, and by following this case, that he's unable –

THE COURT: Who is this doctor?

MR WALSH: Doctor Eileen Tracey.

THE COURT: Doctor Eileen Tracey, the validator? The validator about whom an article was written in the *New York Magazine*, correct?

MR WALSH: If I may finish, your Honor. I've – I've –

THE COURT: Is she a professional, before we go any further?

MR WALSH: It conforms with what I felt before, in essence, when we asked this Court to indulge us, basically from an afternoon proceeding. We cannot put the witness back on in his present state. We want him to receive professional help over the weekend. We're asking that the case go over until Monday morning, at which time we can advise the Court if we can proceed with this witness – if we can ever proceed. We'll have professional opinion at that time. It's in the discretion of the Court. The Court of Appeals has stated in several opinions to grant a reasonable adjournment when someone is ill. In her professional opinion, in dealing with him and in dealing with cases to date, in no way can we put this witness back on to undergo this. We're concerned with the victim of this case. We're concerned about his health and well-being which is paramount and comes first. I would urge the Court to be reasonable and give us an adjournment until Monday morning at ten o'clock. This is a very —

THE COURT: Just so the record is clear: Eileen Tracey is not a medical doctor, is that correct?

MR WALSH: I'm not sure what her exact —

THE COURT: I am sure that Eileen Tracey is not a medical doctor, and I'm sure there was an article about her in the *New York Magazine*.

MR WALSH: Regardless of her, your Honor, we're not asking she necessarily do this, but that someone else does it, and we wish to do this between now and then. That's what we —

THE COURT: I will hear Defense counsel before I make a ruling.

MR KENNEDY: Your Honor, from what I hear from the prosecutor and what I see with my own eyes with reference to Mr Schaefer, it simply does not gel. Your Honor had him on the stand so you could talk to him, to tell him to relax. It's almost over and he seemed fine to me.

THE COURT: It seemed that way to me too.

MR KENNEDY: I'd suggest that he's brought back to the stand again. I have no desire to inflict torment on him, nor does the Court, but my client is being tormented as well.

THE COURT: I am almost inclined to believe, Mr Walsh, that this is a tactic. I do not know what it is, nor do I wish to know, nor what you are trying to compel the Court to do, but this Court is now directing that Mr Schaefer be brought back into this court.

MR WALSH: We'll not produce him in this court because of his physical condition. We cannot continue with him at this time.

THE COURT: All right then, I direct that you call your next witness. The Court directs the Prosecution proceed.

MR WALSH: With —

THE COURT: The Court has observed this young man and has seen no professional from your office who is going to come in here and testify concerning his health. If you wish to bring in some professional I will be glad to hear that professional.

MR WALSH: We would.

THE COURT: I have observed this young man. I know that he has written a letter to you concerning harassment by the District Attorney. That is now in evidence. I observed the young man on the stand. I have found that he answered the questions. I have found that he has been responsive to those questions. I have found that on occasions he has been even more responsive to the questions and anticipated certain questions which were going to follow, and his answers sometimes had to be reduced and some part of his answer stricken. I have found him perfectly capable of answering questions posed by the Court, posed by Defense counsel, and posed by you. Not only have I observed it, but there are in this courtroom individuals — and that is one of the fine reasons that we have media in the courtroom — and it is only a shame that they can only report verbally that which they have seen with respect to this young man answering questions and coming here during the morning recess and appearing ready to go forward. I am now directing you to either call this witness to the stand or to produce some professional who, under oath, is going to testify with regard to his or her ability concerning this witness's ability or inability to proceed with redirect examination. Your failure to do so will cause me to assume that your refusal to put this witness on the stand, your refusal to call any additional witness would mean to me that you have ended the People's case.

The witness has completed his direct and cross. If you so choose not to proceed and do not wish at this particular time to call either a professional or this witness, the Court will assume it is the People's case. I will ask you prior to the People's case whether or not you wish at that particular juncture to make any amendment to the indictment as it now stands. If you do, I will entertain that application, and I will hear arguments on that application. If you do not, I will then have to assume that I must rule on the motion concerning the indictment as it now stands in court and on exactly what it says. If you want some five or ten minutes to confer with your superiors concerning this you may do so. However, I state to you that within the next ten or fifteen minutes either that witness will be on the stand, or some person who physically can examine this witness and state as a professional that this witness is incapable of testifying today, and state the reasons why this witness is incapable of testifying. The Court will do exactly what it says. You make your decisions. I've made mine.

MR WALSH: Is your Honor saying that the People must produce an expert witness in this court in ten minutes and have –

THE COURT: You said you had an expert, you had a doctor called Eileen Tracey who examined the witness.

MR WALSH: I did not say that she had examined the witness. I said that she would like to have someone examine the witness. Obviously we need to have someone look at this witness today.

THE COURT: I've made my ruling.

MR WALSH: We don't have that person here. That's unreasonable.

THE COURT: Either you produce Mr Schaefer or you produce a professional on the stand in fifteen minutes. This Court observed Mr Schaefer, Defense observed him, and individuals in the courtroom observed him. Stop the nonsense and produce the witness.

ME WALSH: Is the Court now –

THE COURT: The Court has taken a recess. You have ten minutes to produce him or produce an expert.

At this point Judge Roberts rose and stormed out of the courtroom, leaving the Defense attorney, quite literally, with his mouth open. Ten minutes later, exactly ten minutes later, he returned and said, 'Call the case,' glaring at the Assistant D.A. as the court clerk called the case.

THE COURT: I will hear you.

MR WALSH: Yes, your Honor. I've asked Karen Andrews to come up. She's our victims' advocate who works in our office and has been dealing with the witness, John Schaefer, for the last day here, and I would like to put her on the stand and ask her a few questions.

THE COURT: Fine. Do so. I might say, before you swear the witness, that in evaluating the credibility of witnesses one considers among other things the inability of witnesses to go forward, and the reluctance of witnesses to go forward. I just state that to the People who are presenting this case. I have also observed the young man.

MR WALSH: The People are aware there's something important.

THE COURT: You are aware of that?

MR WALSH: But there is something more important.

THE COURT: Call the witness.

COURT OFFICER: Have a seat. State your name for the record.

WITNESS: My name is Karen Andrews.

THE COURT: You may proceed, and then I will ask questions.

MR WALSH: Karen Andrews, can you please tell us what your present position is, by whom you are employed, and what your job entails?

A: I'm employed by the Bronx District Attorney's Office as Supervisor of a unit in that office called Crimes

Victims' Assistance Unit. I'm a victims' advocate and have worked in this office for ten and a half years, and I supervise a staff of victims' advocates. We try to provide direct services that are court-related, and related to the needs of crime victims, and in addition we try to support them throughout the court process.

Q: And could you tell us how long you have been doing this?

A: Since September, 1978.

Q: And how many victims have you dealt with in that time?

A: I do not know the exact number. I believe we've had a minimum of one thousand to fifteen hundred cases each year over the past ten years. I must have had direct contact with a large percentage of those cases.

Q: And does that include cases involving victims of sex abuse, and other types of crimes like that?

A: Yes, it does.

Q: Did you ever have occasion to see John Schaefer? Do you know John Schaefer?

A: Yes, I've met John Schaefer.

Q: And prior to today have you seen John Schaefer?

A: Yes, prior to today.

Q: Have you seen John Schaefer today?

A: Yes, I have.

Q: Have you spoken to him?

A: Yes, I have.

Q: And when did you see him? This morning, this afternoon?

A: I've been with him for the last three hours.

Q: Did you see him before he went into court this morning?

A: Yes.

Q: Did you see him when he came back from court?

A: Yes, I did.

Q: Were you able in your experience to make any determination as to his condition when he returned —

MR KENNEDY: Objection, your Honor. With all due respect to Mrs Andrews, I don't know the qualifications of this woman.

THE COURT: Do you have any training as a doctor or psychologist?

A: No, I do not.

THE COURT: What is the extent of your education?

A: I have a university training in art history. I have an extensive personal employment history working as an advocate.

THE COURT: As a victims' advocate that does not preclude you from believing in the presumption of a witness's innocence when a person is charged with a crime?

A: No.

THE COURT: You have occasion, then, when certain victims subsequently turned out to be – not truly to have been victims?

A: That has happened in my experience.

THE COURT: It is so?

A: Yes.

THE COURT: And have you known in the course of your experience individuals who – for want of a better terminology – who were indulging in psychological malingering, and found under this condition a way to avoid proceeding with the matter in hand?

A: I don't have the credentials to make that specific judgement.

THE COURT: If someone says to you that you have the judgement to ascertain when someone says they do not want to testify, that means they are incapable of testifying?

A: I think – I think there are many different reasons why people choose not to testify.

THE COURT: You never hear of people being malingerers in the course of your profession as a victims' advocate?

A: Could you define malingering in a criminal setting?

THE COURT: A malingerer is one that phonies up a condition in order to avoid doing what he has to do. A defendant can be a malingerer if he makes believe that this is a shoe and the shoe is a necktie to phony up a defense of insanity. A malingerer could also be one who wishes to avoid doing what he is compelled to do, and does not wish to do it because it no longer suits him but because it causes him some distress, so he phonies up a condition, be it physical or emotional or mental, in order to avoid that responsibility. Have you ever seen that occur?

A: I would not be able to say that was the cause of an occurrence.

THE COURT: All you can say is that if you observed someone say that they did not wish to testify that that would indicate to you an inability to testify because he is an alleged victim, correct?

A: I find that until we get the cause –

THE COURT: Go ahead, Mr Walsh, you can ask whatever question it is that you want to ask.

MR WALSH: I would like to go back to my original question. Did you observe John Schaefer? Were you able to make any determination as to whether he should, in fact, receive some sort of clinical assistance before continuing to testify?

MR KENNEDY: Your Honor, with due respect I must interpose an objection. She has impeached, if that's the appropriate word, her ability or qualifications.

THE COURT: She doesn't know what malingering is. Maybe she knows what clinical means. You can cross-examine her if you like later.

Q: When you observed John Schaefer return to court today did you notice any change in him?

A: Yes, I did.

Q: What was that change?

A: Mr Schaefer, immediately on leaving this courtroom, was unable – hardly able to stand unassisted. He was crying uncontrollably. His hands – and his body – were shaking for at least half an hour. After he walked out of here he exhibited to me the kind of distress that I've seen in other victims who had passed the point of being able to control their own emotions in a situation that was very, very traumatic for them.

Q: And you as a victims' advocate, what would you suggest had happened to John Schaefer at this time?

A: My concern is that this young man immediately receive the kind of skilled assistance and intervention that we would recommend for anyone in crisis regardless of what brought on the crisis.

MR WALSH: I have no further questions.

THE COURT: Do you know how long this condition will exist – or if it will *ever* end?

A: I cannot answer that question.

THE COURT: You can't answer that? Do you know whether or not any time he is called to the stand his knees will shake, he will cry, and be incapable of testifying?

A: I didn't observe that behaviour on the stand. It was immediately on leaving this room.

THE COURT: Would your testimony be the same if I stated to you that for two whole days he testified and his knees didn't shake, and he didn't quake, and he was in full control of himself, and never exhibited any hysteria on the stand, would that change your opinion with respect to what you observed?

A: No, it would not.

MR WALSH: We are not offering this witness to establish when he would be able to testify, but to the point that he should receive assistance to determine that factor.

THE COURT: Assume for a moment, Mr Walsh, that this embryonic hysteria exists. Now, is a victims' advocate going to come in here on Monday, Tuesday, Wednesday, Thursday, Friday – and I would even open court on a Saturday but never on Sunday – will you then say that the Court will have to adjourn this case indefinitely so that there would be no action in this case, yea or nay, guilty or not guilty, dismissal or non-dismissal, until many eons had passed and the memory of man could no longer recall People against Bernard Lynch?

MR WALSH: I think that comment by the Court is disingenuous. We would suggest that you put the case over to Monday at ten o'clock. I don't think three hours on a Friday afternoon would delay the case that much, and the length of time we have is unreasonable –

THE COURT: Sit down! You talk to the Court and use the phrase 'disingenuous'. You are a little man. A very little man. Not in size or stature but with respect to your ability as a lawyer to respect the Court. You have the audacity to say that to the Court, and I should take action against you, but I won't.

You are standing there and telling me that the witness who testified one whole day on Wednesday, one whole day on Thursday, who appeared to me – although I'm no expert on hysteria nor am I employed by the D.A.'s Office as a victims' advocate – appeared to be able to answer questions that were posed to him. You're telling me that that individual who had all yesterday evening, who had all this morning – you are telling me that this particular individual has quakes in his knees because he was brought up here? I would ask one question of the victims' advocate: You were here before lunch, were you not?

A: Yes, I was.

THE COURT: You were in this courtroom?

A: Yes, I was.

THE COURT: Did you see John Schaefer this morning?

A: Prior to his coming to court?

THE COURT: Yes.

A: Yes.

THE COURT: How long were you with him at that time?

A: Approximately two hours.

THE COURT: Two hours. At that time was he able to stand?

A: Yes.

THE COURT: Was he crying at that time?

A: He was very close to it at several points.

THE COURT: Whether he was close to it or not, was he crying at any time during those two hours?

A: Not openly, no.

THE COURT: Was he participating in conversations with Mr Walsh?

A: Yes.

THE COURT: All right. At the present time where is he located?

A: I believe he is in our office in this building.

THE COURT: For my purposes of assessing him at this particular time I would ask you to please bring him up. If he *is* in that condition I will possibly, after hearing motions, grant a recess. I would like to see him. I would hope in the future, having been a District Attorney myself, that when a person appears to be in a shaky condition we would have the good sense to be able to get a doctor, someone to see him. We do have the number of his psychotherapist who could have seen him during those two hours. If that is the case I would prefer the Court to rely on the testimony of someone who is a psychotherapist or psychologist or a doctor, rather than on someone who has partial training.

MR WALSH: That is our application.

THE COURT: What happened during this whole morning? Why couldn't you have tried to get someone?

MR WALSH: Because in discussing this with the witness this morning I had to make a decision. Our process here is to seek the truth. It is to protect the defendant's rights and those of the victim as well. I made a decision after speaking to him and spending most of yesterday evening with him. I don't think he is in a position to take the

stand and tell the truth because I don't think he is in a position to know what the truth is at the moment. He may never be in that position. I think that in the interest of justice both to the defendant and to the witness that he should receive a clinical examination by someone who is capable of doing it. I simply ask for the case to be put over for that to be done, and have an expert opinion before the Court on Monday.
THE COURT: If the People are of that opinion . . . Mr Walsh, let me ask you this question: If the People are of the opinion at this particular moment that he has an emotional condition which makes it dubious to you as to whether or not – You may step down Ms Andrews, unless you wish to cross-examine, Mr Kennedy?
MR KENNEDY: I wanted to know whether or not Ms Andrews knew that she was dealing with a trained actor, a trained performer?
A: I have known Mr Schaefer for some time.
MR KENNEDY: Do you know he is a trained actor?
A: I have been told that, yes.
THE COURT: Have you observed in the past this same condition, the inability, almost, to stand, the fact that one almost is crying, and the fact that one breaks into tears and expresses unwillingness to proceed.
A: On all the other occasions I have met with Mr Schaefer it's not been related to a court date or a proceeding.
THE COURT: This was the only day that you observed him?
A: Yes.
THE COURT: In view of the fact that you have stated, Mr Walsh, that you are dubious because of the emotional state of this witness to be able to distinguish between telling the truth and not telling the truth, being able to testify in a fashion which would reveal truly that which occurred, and recognizing that in the middle of the examination, and recognizing that you are a representative of the District Attorney's Office

whose interest you have indicated, and the condition of which you speak, is that a condition then that is only brought about by being called for redirect examination or is this a prevalent condition which may exist before direct and during direct, before cross and during cross, and may continue to exist where one shows stress, tears or shakiness, at the prospect of testifying. If that be the case, sir, to quote you, you are 'a representative of the People, here to protect the rights of the defendant and the People, and if a witness appears to me to be so unreliable as being incapable of telling the truth now or on redirect' – that was your phrase, not mine – if that is your evaluation as the Prosecutor in this case, can you, representing the prosecutorial agency, at any time vouch for the credibility of that witness with respect to his testimony before this distress or, indeed, vouch for the credibility of that witness at such time when he does not cry and his knees do not shake? I pose that question to you. It is a rhetorical question. I don't expect an answer.

MR WALSH: I can provide an answer for the Court.

THE COURT: It's a rhetorical question.

MR WALSH: I would like to respond.

THE COURT: I don't care to have you respond, but I would care to observe the young man and ask him a few questions, and if he appears to be in the stated condition then you, yourself, have to search your own conscience, you yourself have to determine and your Office has to determine whether a case in which the image of the District Attorney's Office is more important than proceeding forth with a case and accepting a verdict of guilty or not guilty, a verdict of dismissal or non-dismissal. I would say to you I have felt throughout this trial that it was something which the District Attorney's Office, whether a person is a priest or non-priest, that there are allegations from a person whom I observed on the stand, who answered questions that were posed to him, who expressed as best he could events which transpired. I heard him, and I felt what the District Attorney's Office did was what a prosecutorial office should not do without ruling one way or the other with respect to the credibility or lack of credibility of a witness.

You had a witness, *you* produced him and I felt that an investigation occurred (despite rumors that I have heard and things I have seen) and a case was brought because someone came forward and made a charge which was investigated, a case which you claim was not the product of a conspiracy on the part of the Church, or on the part of the school, or on the part of God knows what, but when I see something like this going on I don't know what the District Attorney's Office is doing at this time.

MR WALSH: We are seeking for the truth.

THE COURT: If you are seeking for the truth, put the witness on the stand and let's get on with it. What is happening here is something which causes people to feel that you have a witness who has absolutely no idea when he is telling the truth and when he is not because *you* have indicated that he is incapable of telling the truth. And this is from the prosecutorial agency. I would merely ask that you bring him up here and I will see what his condition is. If you then press your application and I see that he is incapable of going on, and you insist on putting him up for redirect and putting it over for two days, or three days, or four days, whatever, I'm going to give you enough rope to hang, and this Court is not going to stand up here now and summarily dismiss the case, but I will see the witness, and then I'm going to let you have what you wish in the way of adjournment, and you will have your redirect, and, by God, you will have your redirect if it takes two weeks until his condition is such that he can testify, but you *will* bring him up here. You will *not* get your summary dismissal. You are going to have to stand up like a man and continue with the trial of this case. Now, go down and bring him up.

MR KENNEDY: One application. Because it seems that when Mr Schaefer is in court he is calm and responsive, and when he is in the hands of the Prosecutor's office he begins to quake and quail, I would ask that one of your court officers go along also so that no one can harass him, or abuse him any further.

THE COURT: I will ask a court officer to go down and bring him up here.

MR WALSH: People object to this proceeding. You have attacked the integrity of the District Attorney's Office. I think you should excuse yourself for the fact of your display of anger and hostility to this office. We have indicated that we wish to investigate this matter further. We want him examined further. If *he* can't continue, we can continue the case. If he *can*, we can put him up for redirect. I feel this Court is intimidating the witness. It's his right whether he wishes to proceed or not. We gave him the option to proceed or not to proceed when he first appeared in this courtroom. That letter was written, and he withdrew that letter. It was his decision to go forward, not ours. I think this is totally outrageous for this witness.

THE COURT: Fine. I would like a court officer to accompany Mr Walsh.

MR WALSH: I am not going to bring him up to this courtroom. If your Honor wants to see him in chambers and speak to him there he may do so, but I think it is uncalled for and inappropriate.

THE COURT: Bring him up to the robing room and we'll have both counsels present.

MR KENNEDY: I want to make an observation. The District Attorney's Office is trying to goad you into dismissing this case. They are deliberately trying to scuttle themselves.

MR WALSH: We'll ask for dismissal when we have the full facts.

THE COURT: I will state this to you, sir. I will now ask that the defendant be brought into the robing room, and when *he* is there Defense counsel and Mr Walsh will be there. I will speak to him and then make a determination whether the matter is put over until Monday or whether we proceed. The defendant is to accompany Mr Kennedy and Mr Walsh into the robing room. And I want the complaining witness brought up here too.

It is hard to convey just how dramatic these proceedings had been. When Judge Roberts had bellowed, 'I'm going to give you enough rope to hang,' he had leapt to his feet. And when he told the Prosecutor that, 'By God, you'll have your redirect,' he had slammed a handful of law books on to the desk, making everyone in the courtroom jump. Nobody had ever seen a judge so furious, mostly because he knew that the Prosecution was trying to hoodwink him, and took great exception to the fact. We were fortunate to have Judge Roberts: he was not a man to be intimidated or fooled. He was a stickler for law and truth. These were the two things we wanted, and they were the two things the Prosecution ignored.

The proceedings then moved to the robing room.

THE JUDGE: Mr Schaefer, we have now here the attorneys for the defendant, the defendant, the Prosecutor, the two gentlemen from the FBI, and the victims' advocate.

Now, on Tuesday you came into the courtroom and you took an oath, and on Wednesday you testified the whole day. On Thursday you were on the stand most of the day with the exception that you went downstairs to make some phone calls. You remember that?

SCHAEFER: Yes.

THE JUDGE: It's never pleasant to testify in a case and be subjected to cross-examination, but that is the system under which we operate. In the old days they had trial by ordeal. They would take a guy and put him on the end of a stick and they would dunk him in the water. They kept him under the water, and if he didn't drown he was not guilty, and if he drowned he – well, down he goes. Then they would try by combat where people would get up and flail away at each other with swords. What *we* have is that you answer questions that are posed. Now, I observed you on the stand and you were composed and you answered questions on Tuesday, and you answered questions on Wednesday, and you answered questions on Thursday. There was some problem that existed and that problem concerned itself with a date. Now, a trial is not something where you get a grade on an examination. Your role in a trial is to merely answer the questions that are posed to you, whether it hurts the Prosecution or whether it helps the Prosecution, whether it hurts the Defense or helps the Defense. Your function merely is to get up there and answer the questions. If there is a finding of guilty in this case this doesn't give you a loving cup. If there is a finding of not guilty in this case that is *not* something you have to bear, something that is shameful, or something you did which is wrong.

Under the rules of evidence I have to be convinced beyond a reasonable doubt with respect to the guilt of the defendant. That doesn't mean, for example, if I find someone guilty that you are peaches and cream and the greatest guy that ever came down the Pike. Nor does it mean that if I find someone not guilty that you are a liar, or that you have been telling falsehoods, or that you are evil. Not at all.

The whole purpose of a trial is merely to have you answer questions and see whether or not a witness is able to reach that level, that quantum of proof, which would enable the trier of the facts to find someone guilty beyond a reasonable doubt. The fact that someone points out someone and says, 'That man robbed me, I remember two days ago, that is the fellow,' and picks him out of a line-up, and somehow, during the course of the trial the person gets crossed up or somehow mis-states something and the person is found not guilty – that does not make the person who is the accuser an evil person or burden him with something he has to walk round with as if he had done something shameful. Do you understand what I'm saying to you? It is not such a contest in which your very being depends on the outcome. It is a means by which we settle a dispute, a means by which as best we can, within the framework of our human setting, determine guilt or innocence. Perfect? Not by a long shot. In our system many individuals who are guilty are acquitted because there is a reasonable doubt, and undoubtedly – hopefully, far less – there are individuals who are found guilty who are innocent, and that is the way our system works. It is an imperfect system but it is the system we have. We find it works better than trial by combat, than a trial by ordeal, by some fellow determining in his own mind I've got a feeling, a visceral reaction that somebody is guilty and therefore I'm just going to find him guilty whether he is guilty or not.

SCHAEFER: I'd like to interrupt. I'm familiar with the justice system, how it works. I think this conversation is not pertinent to what's going on here. Really, the point is not whether I'm familiar with the justice system. The point here is that I don't feel physically or emotionally able to go forward with this. I don't. I haven't slept in days. I don't look like this normally. The Defense attorney said to my family he felt I should not go forward as well.

THE JUDGE: When did he say that to you?

SCHAEFER: He said it to my family today.

DEFENSE: I did *not* say that. I did speak with his family.

THE JUDGE: May I say this to you, Mr Schaefer? May I say this to you. You were perfectly well to testify on direct and on cross-examination, correct?

SCHAEFER: No, your Honor, my life is not just in the courtroom. I'm not going to show the whole courtroom how I'm feeling. You put up a façade and that's very strong. Not only is there a façade that's being put there – I'm a very strong person and I can handle this, but I don't think I can use any of my emotional strength to go forward with this.

THE JUDGE: Are you saying to us that you do not wish to testify today, tomorrow, or any other day?

SCHAEFER: That's correct, your Honor.

THE JUDGE: All you have to do is testify now. You know it's redirect which is very, very short.

SCHAEFER: Your Honor, I understand.

THE JUDGE: It is of nothing. It is another fifteen or twenty minutes. A lot of people put a lot of work into this. The FBI Agent worked hard. He has no opinion one way or the other. He gave his evidence. The gentlemen from the FBI worked hard. The detective and Mr Walsh tried to put it together. As did Mr Kennedy and his assistant Mr Cammer. How does it appear? I have indicated to you that it is no shame with respect to testifying and having your position not decided in your favour, but what is shameful is to proceed and then, at the very last moment, very suddenly determine that one is not going to proceed.

SCHAEFER: Based on my physical and emotional condition during the trial, I did not predict this would happen, your Honor. I'm saying I'm tired. I want to go home and I want to put this behind me.

THE JUDGE: You are saying that after testifying for two days you now feel too tired and so duressed you feel you cannot get on the stand at this time?

SCHAEFER: Yes.

THE JUDGE: May I see counsel for all sides, please.

(*Whereupon Mr Walsh, Mr Kennedy and Mr Cammer conferred with the Court, off the record.*)

THE JUDGE: Mr Schaefer, you have put a lot of effort into this matter. You were interviewed. You testified before the Grand Jury. You must have been interviewed in the D.A.'s office. You testified in court. It is a tremendous amount of effort. All that remains, insofar as your role is concerned in this matter, is another short bit of testimony. Are you stating to this Court at this time that you do not wish to testify at all at this time?

SCHAEFER: Yes, your Honor.

THE JUDGE: Are you telling this Court that you do not wish to testify at any time?

SCHAEFER: Yes, your Honor.

THE JUDGE: You do not wish to testify next week or another day next week, correct?

SCHAEFER: No, your Honor.

THE JUDGE: You think if you rested up over the weekend –

SCHAEFER: I'm not going to go through this again, your Honor.

THE JUDGE: Pardon me?

SCHAEFER: I'm not going to go through this physical torture and emotional torture again.

THE JUDGE: This whole thing will take less than half an hour.

SCHAEFER: How do you know that?

THE JUDGE: I know that.

SCHAEFER: No, your Honor, my answer is still the same.

MR WALSH: May I have a moment, please?

THE JUDGE: Do you want to talk to him? Please go ahead. The record should indicate Mr Schaefer is talking to Mr Walsh.

(*Whereupon there was a discussion held off the record.*)

Judge Roberts spent the next half hour or so telling those in the courtroom what had taken place in chambers, concluding by stating that if the Prosecution did not or could not proceed he would have to assume that they had completed the People's case. Finally, he directed his attention to the Prosecution:

THE COURT: After hearing argument from both sides I now turn to you, Mr Walsh, and ask you at this particular juncture what it is you want to do at this point?

MR WALSH: If your Honor please, I have had a conference with Mr Schaefer and I have discussed this with him. He is disgusted with his counselor, and we have conducted a lengthy investigation and extensive trial so far. Although we have full faith in Mr Schaefer's credibility, we believe the fact is that Mr Schaefer can no longer continue in this case, that he is emotionally unable to, and we'll see if we can get some help, some professional help for him. The fact is he cannot continue. It's unlikely he can continue this coming Monday.

THE COURT: May I say one thing. At this particular juncture his testimony is concluded as far as direct and cross are concerned. So far as you have indicated, that would be the People's case, other than the fact that you might want to call insofar as redirect is concerned. Nor would the testimony of Mr Schaefer be stricken because he had both direct and cross. If this is the People's case then it is the People's case because redirect does not constitute a necessary portion of the People's case. If you wish at any time to say that this *is* the People's case, fine, and then you can make whatever application you want.

MR WALSH: No, your Honor. This is not the People's case because we would be required to complete redirect to correct the mistake in the indictment and make an amendment. To do that I would need testimony from Mr Schaefer. I would need to further clarify that date. But I am not confident of putting him on the stand to clarify that at this time.

THE COURT: In other words, what you're saying to the Court is that you don't wish an adjournment to some time next week?

MR WALSH: No, because I think it's fruitless at this point to put the case over. I think we have reached the point of no return. Therefore, I will discontinue the case at this time, and that is the People's position after consulting with Mr Schaefer.

THE COURT: What do you mean by discontinuing?

MR WALSH: I move to dismiss the case in the interest of justice on behalf of the victim.

THE COURT: I will hear you, Mr Kennedy, in view of that statement made by the District Attorney.

MR KENNEDY: Well, it seems to me, your Honor, when the Prosecutor moves at this point to dismiss, it is an attempt to deprive Father Lynch of the vindication he deserves in court. They want to torture him on the one hand and then deprive him of that vindication. I have to remind the Court of a couple of things. I began my examination of John Schaefer – and it is never something an attorney enjoys but I tried to be as pleasant as I could, and he tried to be as forthcoming as he could – and the first thing we learned was that we had a four-page letter written by this young man, in his own hand, saying that in the District Attorney's office, the representatives of the FBI have harassed him, called him names, called him a liar, had cajoled him, had done everything conceivable to get him into court. And finally, apparently, they succeeded, and he said all of the things they clearly meant him to say – which he didn't mean – but they accomplished their task and got him on the stand. Now they want him for redirect examination. I remind you that the word 'disingenuous' was used, and was directed inappropriately at the Court. The disingenuousness of this Prosecution is illustrated by their refusal to say simply, 'We rest', or 'We have no more evidence' or, 'This is all we have and this is all there

169

will be, so let's rest'. Instead of doing that they spend a night with this young man. He presumptively does not say those things they want him to say on redirect, so they come in and tell us now that he is emotionally distraught. I watched you with him, and you watched me with him. We both watched Mr Walsh and Mr Schaefer. He was not comfortable but he was not distraught. He wasn't crying the way he is now. If we have seen the victimization of anyone, I suggest the victimization has been of Mr Schaefer by those individuals who put this case together, and vicariously of Father Lynch for what they have done to him. It is an outrage. We don't want a dismissal on a technicality just because they can't put him up for some silly redirect. Father Lynch deserves vindication. My application is to treat this statement by this statement by the District Attorney as a simple statement of the fact that since they are going no further, therefore they rest. I would make an application for a trial motion of dismissal pursuant to 290.10, and submit it to the Court, and the Court can rule on it. That is the fair thing. They have no more evidence, and they know it, but they hope to be able to walk out of this courtroom and say to the entire world, 'Gee, we had a great prosecution, we had this Catholic priest, but then because of the pressure on this poor young man we could not go forward.' That deprives Father Lynch of the vindication he deserves. That is unfair, and that is abuse.

MR WALSH: We would like this case to continue. We would like to have a verdict. It's quite unfortunate that we cannot. It's unfortunate for both of them. The fact is Mr Schaefer cannot continue. It would be wrong both to him and to Father Lynch. We move to dismiss because we cannot proceed.

THE COURT: This case, without minimizing the allegations contained therein, is far less serious than ninety per cent – and I'm being conservative when I say ninety per cent — of the cases we have in this building involving very serious crimes, involving horrendous murders, and rapes, and robberies where old people are stabbed and beaten. This case is of *some* importance. It has captured the imagination of the media because Father Lynch is a member of the clergy, and because accompanying the trial there were allegations of conspiracies in which the Church was involved. I can say that so far as I am concerned that does not appear to be the case insofar as I have been in the business for forty years and have observed things going on. What we have here is a case which, from an evidentiary standpoint, is not very strong because it is one witness against someone else with no corroboration whatsoever. The young man took the stand and spoke truthfully insofar as all of the evidence is concerned. His direct and cross amounted to the People's case. Mr Kennedy is an able lawyer, as is Mr Walsh. The witness told his story, and the one thing that was attacked was the date. The contention of the Defense was that a fourteen-year-old boy tried to seduce the defendant. It was the contention of the People, on the contrary, that there was an attempt, attempted seduction of the complainant by the defendant. There is no question about the boy being in the apartment, and there appears to be no question either that the young man has some high-strung nature and emotional problem as evidenced by his inability to take the stand today.

One thing I do want to say is what I said to him inside, and that is if someone loses a case — and I address you, Mr Schaefer — if the contentions of the People are not upheld, that does not mean that you are a liar. But I also know what is important to our system, and it is important in our system that you don't dismiss a case on behalf of the victim. When we dismiss a case we say that a defendant is discharged and insofar as the defendant is concerned he is exonerated. In our system for someone to be convicted it is not enough to *suspect* that he may be involved. It is necessary for the People to establish the guilt of someone beyond a reasonable doubt.

The People had an absolute right to go ahead with the prosecution in this matter. I do not attribute to them any evil in which they were trying somehow to attack the homosexual community. That doesn't make sense to me in this age and in this era. I just cannot believe that that is what occurred.

Father Lynch's guilt in this case, as far as the Court is concerned, is based upon hearing all the evidence. Even if a date was finally established for redirect, and if the Defense had rested at that time, I would have denied the motion to dismiss because I would not have felt there was a reasonable doubt with respect to the guilt of Father Bernard Lynch, and I would have found him not guilty and exonerated him. Under our law the quantum of proof is that guilt *must* be established beyond a reasonable doubt. It is not enough to suspect, and I would think that everyone in the law-enforcement community appreciates that and applauds it. That is our way.

Insofar as this case is concerned, for the record, the motion made to dismiss is granted. For you, Father Lynch, as I have indicated, so far as I can see, the entire evidence in this case was completed, and upon hearing all that evidence in this matter, this Court *has* a reasonable doubt, and finds the defendant, Father Lynch, not guilty of the crime.

Finally, the case was over. The gallery, packed with my friends and supporters, religious and lay, heterosexual and gay, burst into spontaneous applause. It was a highly unusual verdict. As Bob Teague was to say, 'At the very end the Judge declared a mis-trial and *then* gave a verdict exonerating the defendant and finding him not guilty. I've never heard of anything like that before.' Michael Kennedy was to put it another way. 'Burton Roberts had the courage – and he's one of the few who has that courage – to face the *facts*, and say publicly as the fact-finder in this particular case, "I find no evidence of guilt here. This man is innocent, and I so find him." That was a courageous Judge.'

Yes, the trial was over, and my vindication was complete. But so many unanswered questions remained that I knew my time of peace was still some way off. Despite the congratulations of my friends, and the champagne party they arranged to celebrate my pyrrhic victory, I still felt shattered by my ordeal. I felt like an old, sick man. I slept very badly that night, and as I tossed I could not help brooding over the way the Church, my Church, had treated me; the way it had forsaken me after I had served it so well and so long; the way the Cardinal Archbishop of New York had, like Pilate, washed his hands of the whole affair; the way a Church that professed itself to be loving and caring showed itself to be neither. It was, I decided, nothing like the Church I had promised to obey.

PART III

A PRIEST IN EXILE

Chapter
Seventeen

In truth I did not particularly care why the FBI and the District
Attorney's Office had targeted me. What I *really* wanted to
know was this: did the Archdiocese of New York have a
role in my persecution? And if so, why? Chris O'Donoghue,
of Channel 9 News in New York, was one of the first to
raise questions: 'Naturally there was a kind of sensationalist
quality in a Catholic priest on a public morals charge against
a minor. But beyond that, it occurred at a time when the
Bronx D.A.'s Office, which was prosecuting the case, was
under investigation itself. Some of their practices and some
of their decisions had come under scrutiny and were found
wanting. So there was that question hanging over them.
And then, of course, the controversial background of the
priest himself, Father Lynch. But when I saw the flimsiness
of the case and how it was presented, I began to ask, why
did they push this case with such a weak witness and such
little evidence? Even the kid himself said he was coerced into
testifying prior to even going to court. So who was pushing
it? And why would they push something that was so shaky
to begin with? Was it a case of bringing a charge that they
felt would never go to court and would, at the same time,
accomplish their goals?'

Or was it as Bob Teague, the WNBC-TV reporter,

believed? 'The man, the target, worked with AIDS patients, gays etcetera. That's what it was all about, and this finally became apparent in the end.'

Everyone who looked into the case came to the same conclusion. 'Father Lynch was a very active political man, particularly here in New York City,' as Michael Kennedy said. 'Because of his ministry to the AIDS victims and because of his championing of homosexual men and women in New York City, he became something of a pariah in the Church. Indeed, we know that the Church sought through a variety of ways within the Church itself to have Father Lynch taken out of New York and returned to Ireland or returned to Africa where he would, it was felt, cause less mischief.'

Robert Cammer, assistant to Mr Kennedy, sees it this way. 'What happened here was a conjoining of related interests. First, I believe that high-level Archdiocese officials were very troubled by Father Lynch's effectiveness, his visibility, and his basic human face. Secondly, we had the unusual situation of an insecure and, dare I say, second-rate temporary District Attorney, Paul Gentile. He had a desire to exploit this case through publicity.'

I have already mentioned SAFE – Students Against Faggots in Education – set up by a small group of students in Mount St Michael's and encouraged by certain members of the faculty whose job it was, as they saw it, to rid Mount St Michael's of gays. Although this bigoted little group consistently denied having any involvement in the action taken against me, there is undeniable evidence that they were deeply involved. It comes from Robert Cammer: 'There is no question that SAFE was active in this prosecution because I saw, when I was in Assistant District Attorney Walsh's office, on the table behind his desk, a file folder with the word SAFE clearly written on it. He turned it over so I wouldn't see the name, but I'd already seen it. Of course, I didn't get a chance to look inside the file.'

Remember that I eventually felt I had to resign from

Mount St Michael's in 1984. But even after I had left, problems at Mount St Michael's continued. The three teachers, Frank Hughes, Albert Poppeti and Joe Pagnozzi, who were instrumental in forcing *my* resignation now focused their attention on the new principal, Brother Timothy Brady, and on some of the other Marist Brothers at the school, claiming that students were being sexually abused by teachers and counsellors. Indeed, Brother Brady was later charged with sexual abuse; he, too, was exonerated. Their animosity towards me, I learned, was still as strong as ever. They blamed me for creating a 'bad atmosphere' at the school which 'continued long after he had left', and tried to get the Archdiocese of New York to come in and 'clean up the school'. Despite three meetings the Archdiocese took no action – presumably because they could find no reason to.

Still not satisfied, or perhaps just frustrated by what he saw as SAFE's lack of success, Joe Pagnozzi telephoned an old school friend, the Assistant D.A., Philip Foglia.

Philip Foglia admits taking such a phone call: 'Naturally, based on his allegations, there was an area of concern, and we felt it was something we should look into. So I called the District Attorney, Mario Merola, and told him what I'd been told. We went over it at length, and then we felt that the appropriate action would be to have someone from our sex crimes unit investigate the allegations.'

But what were those allegations? 'Joe told me that there was widespread homosexual activity at the school that had extended to the abuse of some students there, and that some of the students had been physically abused but at this point were intimidated and were afraid to come forward. In Mr Pagnozzi's opinion some serious crimes had been committed.'

Foglia passed Pagnozzi on to Mitch Garber, a colleague in his D.A.'s office. On June 30, 1987, an important meeting was held at the District Attorney's Office, called by the prosecutors Mary Ann Jennings and Mitch Garber. They had decided to involve the joint FBI/NYPD Task Force on

179

child sex abuse, which was headed by FBI Special Agent Alan McDonald (the same Agent McDonald who was to take John Schaefer for that fateful car ride and 'interview' him). Al McDonald was a staunch and righteous Catholic, Vietnam war hero, and, as he later testified in court, a specialist in child sex abuse. Also present were Special Agent Jim Clementi of the FBI and Detective Joe Gelfand of the NYPD.

With this Task Force set up, Garber said, 'We preliminarily interviewed the three teachers – Hughes, Pagnozzi and Poppeti – and reviewed certain of the documents they had prepared over a period of time. We brought these to the attention of Mr Merola, the District Attorney, and he authorised us to move forward, and to begin to look into the nature of the allegations. They had raised allegations that had implications both in the educational context as well as, arguably, in the criminal context.'

At this stage, according to Garber, none of those three teachers complained about me in the sexual abuse context, only in the educational context. My name was not connected, in their minds, with any possible child sex abuse: 'No such complaint from the teachers at all. Never in fact.'

When, then, did the allegations of sexual misconduct on my part first arise? In Michael Kennedy's opinion, 'When the allegations generally of sexual misconduct were first brought, they were not focused on Father Lynch. They talked about St Michael's in particular. It was not until Father Lynch was focused on by the Church itself and by the Archdiocese in particular that his name began to crop up. As a matter of fact the FBI was the first to bring up Father Lynch's name. It was never mentioned by any of the people they interviewed. So, they targeted him. Why did they target him? I think because he was a political, highly visible man.'

Three weeks into the investigations, John Schaefer made his first appearance. The FBI interviewed him on July 24. But how did Schaefer's name come up at all? He didn't come forward. He had made no complaint to anyone. He was, to all intents and purposes, just another student at the school. So what made the FBI focus on him? Robert Cammer explains, 'We were able to learn that the way John Schaefer was uncovered was through a very difficult – in a sense, hard-nosed – probe by the New York City Police Department, assisted by the FBI. They went to the school with a presumption, a theory, that the school was a hot-bed of homosexuality. That came across in conversations with them and in their notes. The FBI and the police went to students in the school who had been questioned by the three teachers, and they uncovered one student in particular. That student later told me he had been very frightened by the FBI's questioning of him, and he had told them, I don't know anything about what's going on, or if anything's going on, but perhaps, maybe, you could find out something interesting from this fellow, John Schaefer. He's a little bit of an oddball. He has no friends. He hangs out with the Brothers. He only seems to relate to adult men, maybe he could tell you something. There were, that is to say, rumours about him. So he was found by way of an investigation based on rumour, based on speculation, and that led the police to Schaefer. And then he was exploited in the sense that the FBI Agents pretended to be his friends, his buddies, and played up to him, played up to his ego in order to get him on the stand.'

As Kennedy pointed out, the ultimate test of how unfair this investigation was came from Schaefer's own words on the stand. He testified, reluctantly to be sure, but he testified that when the FBI contacted him they had already targeted me, and that at a time when they had no evidence whatsoever. They told John Schaefer that they already had approximately a dozen lads who were willing to give evidence against me. That was absolutely untrue. There was never anyone other than John who said he would testify against me. They also told John that all he had to do was to give them something dirty about me, and then go to the Grand Jury and give his evidence. They told him the case would never go to trial because undoubtedly I would either plead guilty or run away.

But despite their best efforts the FBI investigation ground to a halt in August 1987. Assistant District Attorney Philip Foglia had been following the case: 'Apparently some of the witnesses that Joe Pagnozzi had originally thought he could produce, he could not then produce. There were students he had told us about who either were dissuaded from coming forward by their parents, or who for other reasons did not materialise, and the case was in no way as strong as Mr Pagnozzi had first led us to believe it would be. There was also a problem with the one witness that did come forward and talk to our sex crimes unit. There were severe credibility problems as well as his inability to articulate what exactly occurred, on what dates they occurred etcetera, and that always makes sex crimes very difficult . . . Our office had been through a very highly celebrated sex crimes case, the Praca Daycare Scandal, and we realised the intricacies, and also the impact on the potential defendant, and we wanted to make sure, obviously, that if there was a case to be brought, then it must be brought on very solid ground because it is all too easy to smear someone's reputation.'

The upshot of this was that the District Attorney, Mario Merola, saw the evidence and declined to touch the case: there was no basis for the charges other than the uncorroborated word of a young man, and that certainly wasn't enough.

But D. A. Merola died of a stroke in October 1987. His deputy, Paul Gentile, was appointed by Governor Cuomo to finish Merola's term of office, and Gentile was another matter altogether. Shortly after taking over as D. A., Paul Gentile decided to re-activate the case, and bring the 'evidence' to a Grand Jury. Few who knew Paul Gentile were surprised. Len Levitt of *Newsday* magazine describes him as a District Attorney who was interested in being elected: 'He had been appointed by the Governor . . . on the basis of being the chief assistant, and he was desperate for publicity. He was a man, I would say, who was interested first and foremost in Mr Paul Gentile.'

Paul Gentile has been interviewed about this, and gives his

reasons for re-activating the case thus: 'After a period of time in which it became clear that the potential targets of these allegations had chosen not to testify before a Grand Jury, a vote was taken of the Grand Jurors, which is twenty-three citizens, and Father Lynch and another individual associated with Mount St Michael's were charged with crimes.'

The vote of the Grand Jurors is something of a joke. It was this which Judge Burton Roberts referred to when he said, 'A Grand Jury might very well indict a ham sandwich at the behest of the District Attorney.' It was clear to all that Paul Gentile would derive the maximum mileage from the case.

I was in Ireland at the time the charges were announced at a press conference by the District Attorney's Office on Friday, May 13, 1988. They immediately poisoned the well of justice by making various false statements, such as that I was a fugitive, and that there were *several* allegations from *several* young men. Then they pulled back and tried to hide, leaving me and my supporters to be vilified by the media.

So much for the State organisations, but what about the Church? It transpired that the Archdiocese of New York had allowed the State to defame, prosecute and condemn me, not only without offering me any aid, but also keeping from my attorney information that would have helped me.

I already knew from my encounters in the Phil Donahue Studio that I had incurred the wrath of the lunatic fringe. We know that SAFE had been to the Archdiocese. We know that the 'goings-on' at St Michael's Academy were discussed. The fact that the Archdiocese entirely failed to protect me from the machinations of SAFE could mean that they were willing to see me discredited. Nor were they above getting involved themselves. When a television station described me as a 'fugitive at large', a colleague of mine, Sister Karen Killeen, called the station to tell them that they had got it wrong. I was on holiday in Ireland, not a fugitive. When she asked where this information had come from, she was told, 'From a spokesperson of the Archdiocese of New York'.

They also refused categorically to do anything which might prevent the case coming to trial, something Mr Kennedy wanted in order to minimise not only my distress, but that of the Church too. 'It seemed to me,' he said, 'that part of my responsibility, not only as a lawyer but also as a Catholic, was to try to head off what seemed to me to be the very fateful direction in which this case was going. First I sent a letter, and then spoke personally to an emissary of the Cardinal, suggesting to him that it was in no one's interest that this matter go forward. They made it very clear to me that they were not going to interfere in this prosecution in any way whatever.'

When it came to the preparation of my defence Mr Kennedy was continually balked: 'We knew that the homophobes from Mount St Michael's had gone to the Archdiocese and I wanted to get that correspondence to find out what, if any, activity the Archdiocese had had with reference to bringing these particular charges. I had, of course, subpoenas to get those documents. They immediately got their lawyer – who is a very fine, powerful, prominent lawyer here in town – to move to quash those subpoenas. They said that under no circumstances did they want "Kennedy" to have access to those files. And, indeed, I never did.'

It was a curious and highly suspicious stance for the Church to take. Furthermore many of my religious colleagues, some of them in high ecclesiastical office, sought to solicit support from the officials of the New York Archdiocese. All to no avail; they were treated shamefully, ignored with that arrogance that has epitomised the Archdiocese's attitude towards anyone who dares suggest it might be in the wrong. The Cardinal himself had nothing whatever to say on the subject until a year after the trial, and then his only comment was 'No comment'.

Yet, justice of a sort was done, despite the FBI's persecution and the Archdiocese's silence. It was done in the sense that the truth about my innocence came out for all to see.

One of the saddest aspects of the whole affair was the unrelenting destruction of John Schaefer, who was appallingly victimised by the justice system. He is a very complicated man. He always was a natural and gifted actor, who found playing the extravagant role of victim and witness exciting at first, until he had to face Mr Kennedy in court. He found it difficult and ultimately, to his credit, impossible to lie, and simply pulled out of the role.

Schaefer has been interviewed since the trial, and his statements are revealing: 'I am the type of person who needs to know that people are supporting me. I need to hear the crowd applaud me. I want to know that people like what I've done. I need to feel that what I've done is good. That's one of the reasons why I have a need to be nurtured in my life. I didn't feel it at all in the courtroom. You're on the stand and it was just like the courtroom became a stage. It was crazy all those things, all of the cameras and everything. You don't know how to act.'

One of the saddest episodes occurred when Schaefer was brought to the court for the first time, still protesting that he did not want to testify. He related it himself thus: 'That day I saw Al McDonald when I got to the courtroom, and he tried to calm me down, and he wrote on this little bit of paper, "Sir Galahad", and said, "This is the way you have to face it. It's gone so far there's no turning back now. You just have to go forward and be –" He quoted something from the Knights of the Round Table. I still have that little bit of paper that says "Sir Galahad" on it. He made me feel good about it, whereas everyone else was just trying to push it through.' (Special Agent McDonald, incidentally, died in Scotland three weeks after the trial ended, of a brain tumour according to the New York Times.)

Jim Clementi tried an even more distasteful way of persuasion: 'One of the things Jim Clementi kept trying to push on me was that the same thing had happened to him and he was able – after ten years – he saw this teacher who had raped him, and he was able to bring him to justice afterwards, and it was such a great feeling 'cause he was able to purge his soul and everything afterwards. In retrospect I shouldn't have done this to please other people. I should just have stopped it.'

But John Schaefer was not allowed to stop it.

Chapter
Eighteen

These days I am happy, in joy and in gratitude to God, to declare that I am gay. Even once I had reached the stage where I could admit my homosexuality to myself it was to be years before I felt strong enough to say it publicly, so pervasive and debilitating is the homophobia we encounter in our daily lives. This fear led me into what I now believe was the greatest sin I have ever committed.

The *Late, Late Show* has been running on Irish television for nearly thirty years. Its host – 'Ireland's Pope', some have called him – is Gay Byrne, who runs the show in much the same manner as did Johnny Carson in the States and Terry Wogan in Britain. To be a guest of Gay Byrne is to have 'made it' in Ireland, and when it was first suggested in 1987 that I appear I was keen to do so, because it seemed a good opportunity to bring the problems of PWAs into prominence.

Ed, an Irish gay activist, was a friend of Brigid Ruane, Gay Byrne's research assistant, and an interview was soon arranged. After several conversations with Ms Ruane and Ed it was agreed that no purpose would be served by discussing my own sexual orientation on the show, and it was agreed that the discussion on air would be restricted to my work with PWAs. I was happy with this; my Provincial, not surprisingly, was not particularly enthusiastic about my appearing, though my family were.

The show went out on International AIDS Day, April 8, 1987. I was pleased with the way the interview was going, the way I was getting my points across, when suddenly Byrne turned to me and asked, 'Are you homosexual, Father?' I was devastated by the terrible betrayal. Everything in me wanted to say, 'No, but I *am* gay,' because the word 'homosexual' sounds so clinical, like a medical condition.

But all I said was 'No.' To my eternal shame and chagrin, I had to deny my own creativeness in God. In retrospect it was naïve of me to expect a ruthless pro like Gay Byrne to pass up the sensation a 'Yes' answer would have created, however badly I felt betrayed at the time. Whatever I did or did not admit on the *Late, Late Show*, of course, my very appearance on it was yet another entry in my debit account with the Archdiocese of New York. My work with PWAs had made me a marked man in any case.

I have since been told, by my family and by many members of the gay community, that I did the right thing, that the interview as a whole was successful and valuable. But I have to disagree. My 'No' was a statement of self-hatred, and there will never be freedom for any minority if its members feel compelled, even for the sake of that minority, to deny that they belong to it at all.

The homosexual child is psycho-sexually blinded from birth, trapped in a neurotic cycle of guilt and self-doubt: is it the sins of the child or the sins of the parents which caused this 'abnormality'? From the moment of the first sexual awakening he or she struggles painfully against the heterosexist, homophobic definition of who he/she is. Those of us who are gay know, from experience, how degrading and dehumanising the epithets can be – 'queer', 'faggot', 'fairy', 'pansy' and so on. For so long our prayer was: God, please don't let me be queer. Let me be normal like my brothers, like my friends. You made me like this, and they say I am unnatural, disordered. How can this be? Heal me.'

The hunger for God's approval is built right into the human heart, and cannot be got rid of. Religious conversion, which is the certainty that God loves one for *who* one is, not in spite of who one is, provides the release: the One I love, loves me; I am lovable. To many in the gay and lesbian Catholic community, Dignity was a rite of passage into a self-accepting love in God, a victory over self-rejecting hate. The healing process that began when we said 'No' to society's (and the Catholic Church's) destructive definition of who we were, was hastened by our gathering together to celebrate our God-given gay nature in the spirit of a loving God. And then, when the Church hierarchs drove us out of our church on to the cold winter streets of New York, allowing us not even an inn in which to celebrate Mass, they once again tried to beat us back into our dark, sick closets. With some, they succeeded, and may God forgive them.

The Vatican's 1986 report on the pastoral care of homosexual people had badly stated that the homosexual inclination was an 'objective disorder', and that homosexual acts were an 'intrinsic moral evil'. By extension the Church considers AIDS to be the natural and inevitable consequences of unnatural acts; the gay community has only itself to blame, in other words.

We Catholics can always be forgiven for being sexually active, but never for loving someone of our own gender. Since the Church draws a distinct line between *living* in sin and *committing* sin we are faced with a curious dilemma. People of the same gender who form a loving sexual relationship and decide to live together cannot be forgiven, because in the Church's eyes they are *living* in sin; promiscuous sexual activity is *committing* sin, and hence forgivable. If that is not an incitement to contract AIDS I don't know what is.

It has been my sad experience again and again, especially in my AIDS ministry, to witness the damning effects of my Church's institutionalised God on young people's souls. The Church has, in effect, poisoned their lifeline to God. They have been robbed of the easing of pain that comes with the knowledge that their lives will not ultimately be lost, that human loss is part of some wondrously redemptive design, that the smallest cry of pain does not go unheard. The result, for many Catholic PWAs, is that even in death their spiritual maiming has been so complete that to allow God in would be the ultimate statement of despair; if it comes to a choice between religion and self one must always choose self, because failure to do so is a denial of self and hence a denial of God. Any self-alienation automatically presupposes the alienation of God. As Meister Eckhardt put it, 'Between God and us there is no between.'

As a priest of Christ I am outraged at the murder committed by my Church on the souls of so many people, thousands of whom died from AIDS in darkness and despair because of this inhuman doctrine, the dreadful vacuum being preferable to the poison. At a time when the Church should have been the spiritual home, comfort and solace to these people, it became instead a monster that robbed them of their very souls. 'They had to transcend their Church in order to find their God,' as Sister Patrice Murphy, a Sister of Charity in New York, put it. Many of them failed to do so, and died in awful despair. Worse still, there are documented instances of gay men, dying of AIDS, being refused the sacrament of Holy Communion because they would not renounce their love for their partners – and this at a time when those partners were the only ones to show them that love which they so desperately needed. There have also been cases of priests trying to obtain deathbed 'conversions'.

This relentless homophobia not only fractured the community but devastated many a family. Many good Catholic parents were torn between love of Church and love of children. They presumed that their Church could never be wrong, and were thus, tragically, forced to choose Church before children. I can best illustrate this by quoting the following heart-rending letter, written by a young man from his deathbed to his father. The young man's brother had instructions to publicise the letter if the father refused to read it, which he did, in *PWA Newsline*.

Dad,

I am too weak to write this so I asked Kevin to write it for me. Since you never phone me and hang up when I call you, there is no other way for me to say 'Goodbye'.

When my lover died of AIDS you never expressed any sorrow or compassion. You always treated Dennis like a non-person. That hurt me very much, but nothing can ever compare to the rejection and hurt I felt when you found out I had AIDS and threw me out of the house. I was sick, and your response was to discard me. You never approved of having a gay son. You even told me that no Italian man could be gay. All I ever did know was that I loved Dennis and Dennis loved me. When he died, part of me died with him.

It has been very rough living with AIDS these past three years. Now I know I am dying for sure, and I am ready to go. I want to be with Dennis and with God. He is the father who did not desert me. I'm sure Mom will be waiting too.

Kevin has been a real brother to me. I know he doesn't understand much about being gay, but he has been there for me, and he has even lied and told me that you asked about me. You always knew where I was, so you could have seen me. You were always afraid of what the neighbors and relatives would think if they knew I was gay or had AIDS. You put them before your own son. Kevin tried to defend you, but he always knew that you were wrong.

I am going to a place of peace. Yes, Dad, I believe God is going to welcome me in ways you never did. I have no choice but to forgive you for treating me the way you did. I just wonder if you are ever going to be able to forgive yourself.

I still love you.

Your gay son,

Stephen

Love alone is the absolute, and how to love or be loved should not be preordained by dogma. To deny people the freedom to love in their own way is to say to them, 'I do not believe in you, I do not believe in your ultimate goodness, I do not believe in myself, I do not believe in love, I do not believe in God.'

Those who love to be feared fear to be loved. Most of all they fear themselves. The history of religion is littered with examples of the damage done to the gospel of Jesus Christ by 'guardians of the faith'. Infusing people with fear, and doubt, and guilt, and self-loathing, is far more perverse than any denial of that God of fear, or than irreligiousness itself. I am frightened by the fact that so many Church people find an inhuman, fearful God more acceptable than the transparently *human* face given us in Jesus Christ.

One can hardly ignore, of course, the fact that much modern discussion of religion revolves around what is sometimes referred to as 'religionless Christianity'. The problem of God is man's and woman's problem of God, and we are asked in all seriousness to consider the question of whether Christianity is about God or about being human. The apparently easy answer is that it is about both. The heart of the Christian message is the Incarnation, the humanisation of God, the purpose of which is, within the limits of the possible, the divinisation of the human. Jesus Christ is, according to one of the earliest councils of the Church (Chalcedon), '*verus Deus et verus homo*', both God and man.

A lot of contemporary atheism owes its existence to the conviction that to admit the existence of God is necessarily to restrict the possibility of human freedom and fulfilment. If God exists, is not our freedom reduced by the fact of God, and by the fact that He has apparently made certain claims upon us? Religious people sometimes talk as if they have two distinct commandments to fulfil, to love God and to love humanity, and that the fulfilling of each commandment occupies distinct and separate areas of their time and energy.

It becomes clear, therefore, that the real difficulty in accepting that Christianity is both about God and about being human – *verus Deus et verus homo* – consists not in defining 'God' or 'human', though these are big enough questions, but in knowing what we mean by 'and'. There does not seem to be room for both of us. Either God exists, in which case our space for living and developing is limited, or we are free and God must go. To my mind, if there is any sense to be made of Christian belief, a belief in the God of Jesus Christ, we have to be clear that Christianity is not a new religion: loving God, from which flows a new morality, loving others. Christianity is unique because, in its affirmation of the fact that in Jesus Christ the religious concern and the moral are identified; that in Jesus Christ human concern and human relationships are the disclosure of God; that in Christ God comes to be in humanity in the measure that humanity is opened to His limitless communication. The human possibility becomes, in Christ, the human possibility of God.

In short, Christianity is about the liberating humanisation of God, but in the word made flesh it is we – not God – who are liberated. God is eternal freedom, by plunging Himself into the dark un-freedom of our human misery, by exploding our death into life. Kierkegaard tells a wonderful story of a king who had a divine treasure. Anticipating an attack on his kingdom, he called together his council of elders and asked their advice about where to hide his treasure so that

the attackers would not find it. Each elder in turn suggested a
different place. One suggested the skies; surely no one would
find it there. The king replied that there would come a day
when humankind would explore the skies and there discover
his divine treasure. Another suggested the ocean bed. No, said
the king, there will come a day when humankind will explore
the oceans and there discover my divine treasure. At last a
wizened old woman mumbled to the king, 'Majesty, hide the
treasure that is divine in humanity, and there no one will find
it.' There the king did indeed hide it, and humankind has had
the greatest difficulty in discovering that it is in ourselves that
we most truly find our God.

If each and every one of us is coequally the expression
of God's image and likeness, if we are all, individually
and collectively, the body of Christ, then the Church's
homophobia (and for that matter its sexism) is revealed
for the cruel distortion that it is, with no theological *or*
historical basis. In the earliest Church, when the presbyter
held the host before the communicants saying, 'The body of
Christ', the response, instead of the modern 'Amen', would
be 'I am'. Such was their understanding and acceptance of
their own divine nature through the Christ. How wonderful!
If Christians really believed this, believed that in their human
body-spirits they are the Body of Christ, we would be sexually
freed by our religion, rather than sexually enslaved by it as so
many of us are. No wonder Constantine felt it necessary to
institutionalise this new religion; that kind of freedom for
his subjects was dangerous. There would be, not just in fancy
but in fact, the freedom of God lived out and celebrated in
all people's lives; a daunting concept for those in power.
All chiefs and no Indians, or all Indians and no chiefs, take
your pick.

So, people ask, and I ask of myself, what now? Where do
I go from here? The answer, in fact, is blindingly simple:
it has always been of the utmost importance to me that I
do what I truly believe to be God's will. Obviously being

who I am, being who God created me to be, is the first and only fulfilment of that will. Helping others to be whoever or whatever *they* were created to be is the natural and automatic extension of my doing that will. For over ten years my principal work has been with people who have contracted AIDS, many of whom had been, quite literally, abandoned. Naturally people expected me, as a priest, to have some expertise in dealing with the trauma of death. I have often wondered if my own mother's death wasn't, in some curious way, a gift from God to help me understand death and cope with the death of others. Certainly her death liberated me, in a sense, to pursue what I knew was my vocation: to try to give people the freedom to die in peace with their God, just as she did.

I am often asked how I can reconcile the continued practice of my priesthood with being in a committed gay relationship. The simple answer: in the same way that heterosexual priests who have left the *active* ministry but remain priests (that is to say celebrate mass when and where they are invited to) explain their marriages. The big difference, of course, is that heterosexual priests can receive a dispensation from Rome in order to marry a woman.

Until not long ago I was in a committed relationship. He had been a very real comfort and support in the darkest days in New York, and eventually, after I was given leave from my order, we lived together as a couple. This was an interesting experience for me, because it was the first time I had ever lived so intimately with anyone; it was also awkward, of course, so used was I to being alone. But we learned to love each other and to care for each other; as love grew, so did commitment. We had our difficulties – who doesn't? – but I can safely say that I have never loved anyone more than him. Sadly, our relationship was not to last. Now I live alone, in London, grateful even in the pain of my loss for the experience. I have my work to do, and I know that the God of surprises has something better in store for me.

Epilogue

An Open Letter to His Holiness, Pope John Paul II

'Young people dream dreams, old people see visions.' So it says in scripture. Your Holiness, in the light of what has happened to us, surrounded as we are by AIDS, which kills our bodies; persecuted and tormented by Church authorities who try to take from us our gay and lesbian souls, deny us our human and civil rights, throw us out of our churches, declare our natures 'disordered', our love intrinsically evil, and the typical violence committed against us as 'understandable, if not acceptable', I pray for the day when you, Pope John Paul II, and your successors shall no longer call yourselves the 'Vicars of Christ', realising with all of us that Christ is someone we are all called upon to become – and that this is a process no one achieves in a lifetime, but lasts into and throughout eternity. I pray for the day when your Holiness shall no longer call himself 'Holy Father', but with us and Jesus our Lord realise that no one is good and holy but God alone, and that we have one Father/Mother God, which art in heaven. I pray for the day when you shall lead us into the freedom of the light of disinvestment of all Church monies in racist and unchristian governments; I pray for the day when you shall join the Archbishop of Canterbury, and together

197

ordain the first woman in our Church; I pray for the day when, on bended knee, you go to the Protestant people of Northern Ireland, recognising the Orders of their ministers and the traditions of their churches, so that peace may be possible and justice be done in the country of my birth. Finally, I pray for the day when you shall be the first bishop to defend – extol and defend – the goodness of our instrinsic godliness, in our sexual nature and in the pursuit of our human rights.

Yes, holy Father, I pray. That is my vision, not because the black people are black and women are women, or Protestants Protestants, or gay gay, but because, Holy Father, these people, like you, are co-equally made in the image of our Creator God, our sisters and brothers in the one Lord Christ.